How to Improve Your Assignment Results

How to Improve Your Assignment Results

Colin Neville

Open University Press

Open University Press
McGraw-Hill Education
McGraw-Hill House
Shoppenhangers Road
Maidenhead
Berkshire
England
SL6 2QL

email: enquiries@openup.co.uk
world wide web: www.openup.co.uk

and Two Penn Plaza, New York, NY 10121-2289, USA

First published 2009

A catalogue record of this book is available from the British Library

ISBN-13: 978 0 335 234370 (pb)   978 0 335 23436 3 (hb)
ISBN-10: 0 335 234372 (pb)   0 335 23436 4 (hb)

Library of Congress Cataloging-in-Publication Data
CIP data applied for

Typeset by RefineCatch Limited, Bungay, Suffolk
Printed in the UK by Bell and Bain Ltd, Glasgow

Fictitious names of companies, products, people, characters and/or
data that may be used herein (in case studies or in examples) are not
intended to represent any real individual, company, product or event.

The **McGraw·Hill** Companies

Contents

Acknowledgements

In many respects this is the most important section of the book. People who give freely and generously of their time and experience often do not realize what valuable support they give to others and I would like to thank the following for their contributions to the development of this book:

To my wife, Wendy, for her careful proofreading of the book and her many suggestions for amendments and improvements to the text.

Dr Greta Defeyter, Northumbria University, for indirectly encouraging me to write this book. A booklet I wrote for the School of Management, University of Bradford: *Your Assignment Results and How to Improve Them*, received positive reviews from Dr Defeyter's students and gave me an incentive to develop the themes in the booklet into book form.

Professor Lin Norton, Liverpool Hope University for her permission to use the tutor expectations exercise in Chapter 2; and for Lin Norton, Edd Pitt, Katherine Harrington, James Elander, and Pete Reddy of the 'WriteNow' Centre of Excellence in Teaching and Learning (CETL) network, for their permissions to use extracts and quotations from their excellent publication: *What I Wish I Knew in My First Year About Writing Essays at University*.

MBA and MA students at the University of Bradford, School of Management, 2006/07, for their comments that are shown, with their permission, and especially to Mr Satyajit Sharma, whose wise comments I particularly admired.

Tracy Johnson, Education Support Unit, University of Bristol, for her helpful insights that influenced Chapter 3 of the book.

Former School of Management, University of Bradford, colleagues: Dr David Spicer, Dr Jenny Fairbrass, Dr Peter Morgan, and Dr Deli Yang, whose past written comments to me I have gratefully included in the opening chapters.

Colleagues: Becka Currant, Russell Delderfield, and Michael Cross at the Learner Development Unit, University of Bradford, for their permission to use extracts from their learner support resources and materials.

Martin Sedgley, Effective Learning Adviser, at the School of Management, University of Bradford, whose counsel on all matters affecting student learning I trust and value.

Steve Cook, Fellowship and Education Officer, the Royal Literary Fund (RLF), for permission to use the extract from the RLF publication: *Writing Matters*, which is shown in Chapter 10 of this book and presented as an example of effective writing.

Why read this book?

Flight • Fright • Fight • What this book covers • What to expect in each chapter

If you are an undergraduate or postgraduate student and have had disappointing results for your course work assignments – but want to improve your future grades – this book is for you.

It can be unsettling and upsetting if you receive unexpectedly poor grades for course work, as criticism aims a sharp blow to one's self-image. A whole range of emotions are evoked, including disappointment, anger, frustration, and depression. Students can lose confidence in themselves as learners when they do not receive good marks and appreciative feedback from tutors.

For many people, praise has come regularly to them throughout their lives, particularly from parents, and later from teachers or employers. This can lead to confidence and self-assurance – but also a degree of complacency. When criticism does come, it can shake and rock the pillars of their self-esteem in an alarming and disorienting way.

For others, this early praise and support may have been inconsistent, missing, or grudgingly given, so the growth of confidence has been much slower for them. It may, however, have laid down sufficient layers to support their application to higher education, but the thin veneer of assurance is easily stripped away by poor assignment results.

The ability of an individual to respond positively to unexpected criticism depends in large measure on the support received from others, and on the inner resources of the person to cope with this setback. When faced with course work results that are unexpectedly poor, individuals are likely to respond in one of three main ways: flight, fright, or fight:

- Flight: think of quitting the course.
- Fright: don't do anything in the hope that things improve.
- Fight: look for ways to do better next time.

Flight

Quitting can be an easy option; it can lead to an immediate surge of relief and a lightening of the emotional load. And it can be the right response if you honestly feel you are on the wrong course. Sometimes course work goes badly because you want it to. You may not have wanted to be on that particular course in the first place. It may have been an expedient rather than heart-felt choice, chosen for ill considered career related reasons, or because another person felt it would be a 'good' move for you – or them. In your heart you may have known it was not right for you, so your poor results prove it – and give you a way out. This can be positive in the long term if you pursue other learning or work opportunities that suit you better.

However, if the course is generally OK and can take you towards a lifestyle or career that will suit you, the option of flight is likely to be an unwise choice. It may lead to long term emotional consequences, often in the shape of a battered self-image and lack of confidence to take risks in the future. Flight may become a bad habit in the face of difficulties.

Fright

Fright means doing nothing. It means adopting a head-in-the-sand approach to difficulties. You probably hope that the poor result is a temporary blip in the scheme of things and that all will be well in the future. This might be the case, but equally it might not – and in your heart you are likely to know that problems lie ahead unless you do something to address the difficulties that have become apparent.

Fight

The chances are that you are reading this book because you are shrewd and strong enough to recognize that a poor course work result is not a damning verdict on you as a human being, but a transient comment on your past work.

So this book is a 'fight' style book to address the reasons:

- Why and where you went wrong with your course work assignments.
- What the tutor's comments really *'mean'* – they may not always be clear – or may have been misinterpreted by you.
- What you can do to improve your results in the future.

What this book covers

The book covers the preparation, writing, and presentation of course assignments in the forms of:

- Essays.
- Reports.
- Dissertations.

Exams and tests are not covered, although the techniques and ideas outlined in many of the chapters, particularly 3 to 6, will certainly be relevant to passing exams.

What to expect in each chapter

This section will give you a quick overview of what you will find in each chapter. I suggest you read Chapters 1 and 2, and then pick the others that seem to connect with the type of assignment feedback you have been receiving from tutors. The final chapter is also recommended reading, with sources of support that may help you in the future.

Chapter 1 The shock of poor results

This opening chapter looks at the impact of poor results generally and draws on the experiences of undergraduate and postgraduate students on dealing with the shock and disappointment of poor results. It asks you to think about your main and recurring assessment related concerns.

Chapter 2 Interpreting your assignment results

The aim of this chapter is to explain what tutors are looking for in assignments, and about UK marking criteria at both postgraduate and undergraduate levels. It highlights the general features of assignments which achieve 'highest', 'good', and 'low' marks.

Chapter 3 'You have not answered or addressed the question'

This is the first of the seven chapters with titles that use common tutor feedback comments to help you identify the relevant chapters to read. The aim of this chapter is to interpret and explain what is meant by comments of this type, and what you might do to address the issues raised.

Chapter 4 'Your work is more descriptive than critical'

This criticism is often the most baffling to many students who do not understand the comment and what is expected of them. The aim of the chapter is both to explain what is meant by 'critical analysis', or 'critical thinking', and to show what is expected of you.

Chapter 5 'Your assignment was poorly structured'

This is a very common criticism, but students are often not sure how to rectify the problem. The aim of this chapter is to explain and illustrate, with examples, what is meant by 'good' and 'poor' essay and report structure. It also presents you with a framework that can be used for planning and structuring ideas and will include a short essay and a report to illustrate how good structures can be achieved.

Chapter 6 'You did not tell me anything new'

This criticism occasionally occurs and can confound students, particularly those who are used to faithfully reproducing what they have been told by tutors. The aim of this chapter is to explain what is meant by this type of criticism and to show how you might respond to it by becoming more creative with ideas and in their presentation.

Chapter 7 'Your reading for this assignment is limited'

Students can be criticized by tutors for not consulting sources outside of those on recommended reading lists, or for using the Internet in an undiscriminating way. The aim of this chapter is to explain why tutors make these comments, and the range, reliability, and validity of sources for evidence in your assignments will be discussed. A framework for evaluating the credibility of websites will also be presented.

Chapter 8 'You need to improve your referencing'

Poor referencing practice is often linked with the difficulties students have generally in managing and using evidence in assignments. The aim of this chapter is to explain the principles underpinning referencing, when sources should be cited and referenced, and how to avoid plagiarism. You will be presented with examples of how to cite and reference sources using the main referencing styles applied in higher education institutions in Britain today.

Chapter 9 'Your English is weak: it was difficult to follow your arguments'

The aim of this chapter is to present and illustrate the three most common writing problems encountered and criticized by tutors: (a) overlong and convoluted sentences; (b) common grammatical errors, particularly regarding the use of the comma and the apostrophe; and (c) commonly confused and misspelt words that can outwit the spell checker on your personal computer.

Chapter 10 Finding your own voice in assignments

Many students when they enter higher education are confused about a gap they perceive between the conventions of academic writing and the need to make points in essays in their own individual ways. Your tutors will want you to remain objective and to draw on a range of authors and their arguments. But they also want to see authenticity and individuality in your writing and not a cut and paste fusion of a dozen other people's words and ideas. This chapter will look at how to present ideas persuasively and in an individual way, but still stay within the expected conventions of academic writing.

Chapter 11 Sources of help

This final chapter will outline sources of help and support for you, including peer assisted learning, 'study buddy' schemes, counselling services, personal tutors and learner support units, and the work of **LearnHigher**, **Write-Now**, and other Centres of Excellence in Teaching and Learning (CETL). It will also discuss the benefits of keeping a learning journal to improve your future assignment results.

1

The shock of poor results

Impact • Moving on • Self-analysis

This chapter is about:

- The shock of receiving poor assignment results.
- The importance of identifying recurring problems.
- Having a plan to improve future results.

Once upon a cob-webbed time, I was a part time student and still in the early stages of my degree course. Having marked our first assignment the tutor announced individual results to the whole tutor group. I was told publicly that I had 'not answered the question', so had failed the assignment.

My first reaction was disbelief, then shock, followed by anger, quickly pursued by humiliation, and all these compounded by the barely concealed smirks of my fellow students. I sat in stunned silence for the remainder of the first half of the class. At break I was avoided by other students as if my failure was contagious; or perhaps, more likely, I avoided them, to escape the expressions of 'sympathy' I believed they did not really feel.

Fast forward the scene now to the present time and to the reaction of a twenty-first century student on receiving similar news. Bad news may be more sensitively delivered now, but the emotional impact can be just the same. One student wrote to me to say:

Results came and I got the most dreaded word in a student life 'E'. I was hit and hit very badly; before I could realise what went wrong I was hit by the result of my second assignment: "D"; slightly improved but still nowhere near good. I was hit with all sorts of pessimism surrounding me from all over.

I have been conscious for many years of the impact of poor assignments results, and when I started researching for this book, I e-mailed students at the Management School where I worked asking how they felt about, and managed, disappointing course work results. Normally, I might expect half a dozen students to respond to such a request, but this time I quickly received over two dozen replies. My message had touched a raw nerve in their lives. Many of the student quotations in this book are from this correspondence, and I also include written comments from tutors in the same school. Quotations from other sources are cited and referenced.

1.1 Impact

The word 'hit', used repeatedly by the student in the previous quotation, describes aptly the impact of such criticism and just how it feels. Poor results strike hard at your pride, your self-esteem, and your confidence. Unexpectedly bad results in course assignments, or critical feedback comments from a lecturer, can have a profound impact on the morale and motivation of students. This can not only affect the classification of their degrees, but can lead to depression, anxiety, and even early withdrawal from a course.

Evidence that some undergraduate students can be particularly badly affected by negative feedback comments was found by Young (2000). One student was quoted as saying: 'It's a personal thing, and I think that because now I've come back into education and it's the first time that I've done something academic really. Now I've put that value on myself, my value is that I'm good at this. So if I get criticised, the value's taken away' (p. 414).

Ravi Rana, a student counsellor, also describes the reaction of an undergraduate student criticized by his tutor for 'not reading the question' properly:

> . . . he had felt that his tutor considered him to be 'completely stupid' and that he had felt himself fill up with panic and had been afraid that he might cry in front of other students in his class. When asked, he was able to recall that the tutor had made similar comments to several other students, however, this did not diminish at all his sense of being especially insulted or help him to put his own experience into perspective
>
> (Rana 2000: 133)

Young felt that the impact made by tutor comments depended on the level of self-esteem felt by the students. If a student's self-esteem was low, even tutor comments intended to be helpful could be perceived as negative and could have the unintended consequence of sending the student into depression. The student concerned may have invested a lot of emotional energy into returning to study, which can make them particularly vulnerable and ultra-sensitive to criticism. On the other hand, Young commented that 'students with higher self-esteem started out with a positive attitude to being assessed and receiving criticism' (2000: 412). They subsequently treated any criticism as opportunities for improvement, rather than as damning critiques of their abilities.

However, for many students, and particularly international students, the consequences go beyond self-esteem to affect personal finances and to impact on other family members. One of the students who contacted me wrote:

'we have spent around 10,000 pounds [to study on the course] but after spending that if we are still not able to get this degree then how can we face our family? I was totally sure that I would pass all assignments, but it has not happened . . . the studies criteria here and in our country is very much different'.

Another wrote about feeling 'cheated', as if his investment both in time and money had not paid off: 'Got a "C". I felt cheated! Couldn't work out where I went wrong. I attended all lectures and tutorials, read all text and really enjoyed the subject. As such I studied really hard . . .'

Another student expressed his initial feelings of disbelief and then feeling of isolation on receiving his disappointing results:

'In the beginning when I got my disappointing mark, I said "it is not mine"! It was really disappointing and it took me a while to get out from this; I didn't find anyone to talk to. No friends will understand the situation and circumstances you have been through'.

These feelings of disbelief, shock, and hurt to self-image can be experienced by undergraduate and postgraduate students of any age and regardless of social class, gender, and cultural boundaries. They are compounded by a mix of internal feelings and external factors:

Internal feelings	External factors
• You may feel that your self-image or identity is under threat. • You may question your level of general ability or motivation. • You may be confused or baffled about how to do better in future assignments.	• You may not have much, or any, previous experience of course work as a means of assessment. • You may feel responsible for lowering a group mark because of your contribution to an assignment. • You may become worried about your overall module or course results. • You may feel that your long term career prospects are threatened. • You may feel you are letting others down, particularly family members.

1.2 Moving on

However, all the students who contacted me had adopted the 'fight' rather than 'flight' approach. Their will to learn and motivation to succeed was strong – and helped them rise above their initial feelings of rejection and disappointment. Their 'fight back' tended to show a recurring pattern of reflection and action, which usually involved one or more of three responses:

• Self-analysis.
• Seeking advice from tutors.
• Seeking help from other sources.

1.3 Self-analysis

The issue of seeking advice from tutors and from other sources will be the subject of a section in Chapter 11, but at this point it is enough to say that discussion with tutors is an important element in improving your future assignment results.

Self-analysis generally involved among these students an honest self-appraisal of what had gone wrong. One student wrote: 'At night, or whenever my head is clear, I would review my mistakes carefully, make a note of them and be hopeful to do better next time'.

Another commented on his gut feelings that his work was not 'quite right':

Originally I felt disappointed. However, I soon realised that the paper could have done with more independent reading. I resolved to actually take the feedback advice on board and do more reading for the next paper. I must say that, if I receive a disappointing grade, I usually know, somewhere in my mind, that my paper isn't 'quite right'. So I also resolve to rely more on my instincts and improve a paper before handing it in if I am not fully satisfied with it.

One way of beginning to analyse the problem is to ask the questions, 'What are the difficulties (or recurring difficulties) in my work? Are there any common themes from the feedback I receive from tutors?' You can use the space that follows to write your responses to these questions.

Common and recurrent criticism

How you can begin to resolve the issues you raised is dealt with in later chapters of the book. For example:

You don't really understand what's expected of you in assignments:	Read Chapter 2.
Tutors say you are failing to answer the question:	Read Chapters 2, 3, and 6.
You are not clear in your mind on differences between description and analysis:	Read Chapters 3, 4, 6, and 7 – although others, for example 10 and 11, will also be helpful.
You find it difficult to write in a well structured and organized way:	Read Chapter 5.
You are not sure when, why, or how to reference sources:	Read Chapter 8.

Your sentences are often over-long, and/or you have problems with punctuation and spelling:	Read Chapter 9.
You struggle to express your own ideas in an 'academic' way.	Read Chapter 10.
You are not sure who can support and help you gain better assignment results.	Read Chapter 11.

Main points from this chapter:

- A judgement on your work is not a judgement on you as a person.
- Don't run away from or ignore the problems highlighted in tutor feedback.
- Look for recurring feedback comments from tutors.
- Talk to tutors about poor coursework results – get their advice on exactly what was wrong and how you can improve (see Chapter 11 for more information).
- Look for additional sources of support (see Chapter 11).

2

Interpreting your assignment results

Essays and reports • What the marks from your tutors 'mean' • What tutors expect of you

This chapter is about:

- The difference between essays and reports.
- What the marks awarded by your tutors 'mean'.
- What tutors expect of you in assignments.

2.1 Essays and reports

Written assignments generally fall into two broad types: essays and essay style assignments, and reports. What's the difference?

Essay	Report
An essay requires you to think and write about ideas. These ideas are often presented in the form of a question or statement for you to analyse. Essays can allow you to explore hypothetical situations and to expand on possibilities, ideas and concepts.	A written report is a factual and systematic account of a past event. A report will often make recommendations, but an essay will rarely do this.

The English statesman, Thomas More, wrote an essay entitled *Utopia*, which envisaged an ideal state or perfect world. He could not have written a report on the same topic!

There are presentational differences in the way you actually write essays and reports, although in some subject areas, a hybrid style of writing is allowed. I am stressing this point because if you are asked to write an essay, you need to be clear what form of writing is expected of you; similarly with reports. Not writing in the appropriate style may be contributing to your problem!

2.1.1 Essays

A traditional style essay is most usually characterized by ideas and comments grouped into paragraphs and without subheadings, bullet points, or graphs and charts, which are a feature of many reports. However, this general rule is not universally applicable to all disciplines, and some tutors on some courses, e.g. business and management, will not object if you add subheadings or bullet points to an essay. Indeed, some essay topics, particularly in the more technical subject areas, are better suited to report-style writing formats. You need therefore to check with your module tutor what style of writing is acceptable.

Ask them:

- Do they expect a traditional style of essay, without subheadings and bullet points?
- Or would they **prefer** it if you added subheadings and bullet points to your essay, in a report-style format?
- Or don't they mind – is either acceptable to them?

Example

The following is an extract from the opening section of an **essay** written in a traditional style. The ideas are broken into paragraphs, but the paragraphs are not given subheadings. Each paragraph focuses on a particular idea. The first paragraph shown here introduces the essay to a reader; the second defines and explains a key term, 'life planning':

What advice would you give an organization concerning ways they could introduce and implement life planning? Support your answer with reference to theoretical and practical evidence and argument.

This essay will define the term 'life planning' and present the advantages for employers of introducing life planning support for their employees. One of the biggest obstacles to the introduction of life programmes for employees is to offer convincing reasons to organizations as to why they should do it at all. The essay will, therefore, address the, '*What's in it for me?*' question that employers ask.

Assuming these answers did prove satisfactory to an employer, the ways they could introduce and implement life planning will be discussed. A significant point that will be made is that more research needs to be done on the impact of life planning programmes on the motivation and performance of employees in order to convince employers of their value.

Life planning is a process to encourage people to review their lives, identify life priorities, consider options and make plans to implement choices (Coleman and Chiva 1991). It is an idea that started in the USA, but has found its way to Britain and the rest of Europe in recent years. Hopson and Scally (1999) suggest the process is built on seven life management skills: knowing yourself; learning from experience; research and information retrieval skills; setting objectives and making action plans; making decisions; looking after yourself; and communicating with others. They argue that these skills are necessary to avoid 'pinball living': where individuals are bounced from one situation to another without any clear direction.

2.2.1 Reports

The following is an extract from the first page of a **report**. There are sub-headings for each section and bullet points are used:

Example

Introduction

This case study report examines the range of work activities in the UK that can be classed as Tele-working and, in particular, work from home and work in call centres. It will summarize the age and gender profile of workers in the sector and the advantages and disadvantages of Tele-working generally. In recent years there has been speculation about the future of jobs in the UK call centre. A significant proportion of this report will examine the future of, and the challenges facing, this particular occupational area.

Types of Tele-worker

There are two types of Tele-workers:

- Those who work at home or use their home as a base at least one day a week using both a telephone and computer; and
- Those who work away from home in a call centre or another form of collective work base.

Extent of Tele-working in Britain

A study in the mid-1990s (Huws 1996) attempted to discover the extent of Tele-working in the UK and assess the potential for expanding work of this nature. The findings from this survey are summarized as follows:

- 5 per cent of the British workforce can be defined as Tele-workers;
- Of these, 68 per cent are male, 32 per cent female;
- 41 per cent of female Tele-workers work at home, compared with only 15 per cent of men.

2.2 What the marks from your tutors 'mean'

You should always ask for marking criteria from your tutors, if they are not automatically given with assignments. But do you really understand what a C grade, or mark in the 50–59 actually 'means', in terms of its verdict on the quality of work you submit? Many students, particularly international students, are often disappointed with the marks they receive for written assignments, and a C grade is often regarded by them as very low. But in Britain the majority of students will achieve marks of between 55–65 for their assignments (between a mid-C to mid-B range). A mark of between 65–69, or a top B grade, is considered as a very good achievement for assignments.

This may contrast with typical pass marks in other countries, where 60–65 is regarded as a baseline, and 70 regarded as an acceptable lowest point. In Britain, however, a mark of 70 or over would be reserved for students whose work is significantly above average.

You can draw an analogy between your results and a journey. The following is adapted from an article by Skok (2003).

1st class (70+)   **A** grade work: the **explorer**

The **explorer** has pursued the subject in a very thorough, and perhaps even a creative way (see Chapter 6). The explorer will be brave enough to venture into academic 'territory' others have not. For example, the explorer may have demonstrated a willingness and ability to be creative with established ideas or practices in a thorough, analytical, and objective way. The explorer may also have made connections between different ideas and concepts and presented an original perspective on the subject.

Features of the work submitted:

- The work will be of a **distinguished** quality, is based on extensive reading that demonstrates an authoritative grasp of concepts, methodology, and content.
- There will be clear evidence of originality of thought, as well as an ability to synthesize complex material and to think analytically and/or critically.
- There will be evidence of reading beyond the set texts.
- The work will also be presented to a high standard, without spelling and grammatical errors, and with accurate referencing.

Two tutors advised me on their specific criteria for awarding an A grade; their comments would certainly be echoed by many others:

There are six things I look for to justify a mark of 70+.

First, I look for critical analysis and argument. This means I am looking for evidence of the student's own thinking; their own criticisms of the main issues, but done in a detached and objective way.

Second, there should be clear evidence to support ideas presented, and evidence gathered from a range of sources, such as statistical analysis and case studies.

Third, the student should connect with the assignment topic – and answer the set question.

Fourth, the presentation of the assignment should be above average, in terms of good structure, clear introduction, very good conclusion, clear and succinct writing, without spelling mistakes, plus good flow and linkages between paragraphs.

Fifth, the references must be correctly presented, with citations in the text and a list of references presented at the end of the assignment in the correct way.

And finally, there should obviously be no plagiarism, and, above all, I ask myself: 'has the student read and followed accurately all the assignment instructions and guidelines'?

(Tutor 1)

I am looking for demonstration of four main skills:

1 **Description**: This includes understanding of content; knowledge of models, tools and theory, including the main commentators on a particular topic.
2 **Analysis**: This can include questions on the topic, such as why? Why not? Plus demonstrating knowledge of cause and effect relationships.
3 **Evaluation**: This is about weighing things up, for example pros/cons; advantages and disadvantages; ranking; strengths and weaknesses.
4 **Synthesis**: This is essentially about bringing it all together in a coherent way, so takes into account structure, flow, logic. It also includes making arguments, and the use of data/evidence to arrive at conclusions.

(Tutor 2)

2.1 class (60–69) **B** grade work: the **traveller**

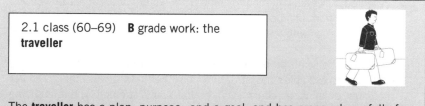

The **traveller** has a plan, purpose, and a goal, and has prepared carefully for the assignment 'journey'. The traveller, with more effort and confidence, could easily become an 'explorer'. It will certainly be above average work, but just lacks that vital spark, insight, or demonstration of wide reading that can push an assignment into an A grade. Nevertheless, a B grade, particularly in the top range, equates to very good work: work to be proud of.

Features of the work submitted:

- This will be work that demonstrates a sound understanding of concepts, methodology, and content.
- Towards the top end of this range there is likely to be clear evidence of critical judgement in selecting, ordering, and analysing content.
- The work shows the relationship between different issues or concepts and presents evidence and examples to support arguments and main points.
- The work will be well organized and written with good grammar, correct spelling, and accurate referencing.

2.2 class (50–59)   **C** grade work: the **tourist**

The **tourist** likes to play safe and not take any risks. Although the tourist has prepared for the assignment, they quite like to be told what to do, rather than discover things for themselves. The tourist will report back accurately on what he or she has read, but will not explore too far, or at all, 'below the surface' of a subject by, for example, making wider or deeper connections between theories, models, or practices, or by challenging ideas.

Features of the work submitted:

- The course work is derived from a reasonable to good foundation of reading and it is likely to demonstrate, in an adequate way, a grasp of relevant materials and key concepts, as well as the ability to present points of view in a clear way.
- There are no serious omissions or irrelevancies in content. Examples presented, however, will tend to come from lecture notes or set text books, rather than from independent reading. The tutor is likely to say 'OK, you have got to grips with the main ideas, but there is nothing new or different here'.
- There may be some problems in the way the work is organized and presented. For example, the structure may be a little disjointed, and/or there may be minor inaccuracies in grammar and spelling. The referencing may also be flawed in parts; for example, evidence may not be cited and referenced correctly.

3rd class (40–49) **D** grade: the **wanderer**

The **wanderer** may occasionally be en route to a destination, but often is not. In a particular assignment, for example, he or she may have wandered off the track or point, or not really understood where they were 'going', or the 'destination' or main point of view was unclear.
Features of the work submitted:

- The course work shows only a partial understanding of key concepts and limitations in the selection of relevant material.
- The work may be flawed by some significant omissions or the inclusion of irrelevant material.
- Few or no examples are offered to illustrate ideas.
- The work may be poorly organized and structured.
- There may also be a noticeable number of spelling and grammatical errors.
- The work is also likely to be poorly referenced.

At undergraduate level this work will scrape though, but the tutor is likely to write something along these lines about the work: 'Although you show enough understanding of the subject to pass, you have not really engaged with the set question. It was more a collection of facts assembled together with no real effort being made to use them in addressing the question'.

Fail (below 40 – or 50 for postgraduate study): **lost**

The **lost** student either had not worked out clearly enough where he or she was going, or became quickly 'lost'. In assignments, the lost students are generally those who have not understood what was expected of them, or thought they knew where they were 'going' – but clearly did not! The lost students are those who did not answer the question, or answered it very badly. But like anyone who is 'lost', the student can get back on the right track with some help and direction.
Features of the work submitted:

- The student has either not addressed or not answered the assignment task or question.
- There is likely to be substantial generalization, suggesting that knowledge of basic ideas is limited or completely lacking.
- There is little, if any, evidence of reading and independent thought on the subject.
- The organization and structure of the work is poor.
- The standard of English in the writing may also be weak, making ideas hard to follow or understand.
- There may also be evidence of plagiarism and/or poor referencing practice.
- The tutor has simply not found enough in the assignment to deem it worthy of a pass.

2.3 What tutors expect of you

So far in this chapter, you have been introduced to the broad criteria that tutors use for marking assignments, and you have read comments from some tutors on when and why they would award an A grade. But there are thousands of tutors out there, working in hundreds of different disciplines, so is it possible to generalize about the criteria they adopt for marking your assignments? The answer is both yes and no.

The answer is 'yes', in the sense that there are some recurring elements that appear to cross discipline boundaries; but it is 'no' in that you need always to ask an individual tutor what their criteria is for marking your work, and what their general expectations are – as tutors can vary in the elements they prioritize. Assessment criteria are the elements that tutors seek to find in your assignments to judge how well you have learned. The chances are that the criteria will be supplied to you in individual module or course guidelines. But if they are not, then you should always ask the tutor for them.

Some studies have looked at how tutors in the same departments mark assignments. For example, a study by Norton (1990) of the assessment criteria in a department of psychology identified a range of assessment criteria and asked staff to rank these in order of importance.

Exercise

Try and work out for yourself what the result was. Mark the criteria you think is most important as 1; the second most important 2, and so on.

Criteria	Rank
Clear structure and organization	
Answers the question	
Accurate use of English	
Effective presentation and writing style	
Demonstrates understanding of the subject	
Evidence and demonstration of wide reading	
Relevant information is selected and used in the assignment	
There is a clear point of view or 'argument'	
Evaluation of evidence (ability to identify strengths and weaknesses of what you read)	

Now look at Appendix 1 for the result of this study.

2.3.1 Four main concerns of tutors

Clanchy and Ballard (1998) have argued that there are four main areas of performance in essays about which many tutors hold clear expectations. The four tutor expectations are:

1 *Relevance to the set topic.* The tutor will expect that your essay will be focused on the topic and, if the essay is presented in the form of a question, that this question is clearly addressed. The tutor will be looking for evidence of your understanding of the knowledge that underpins the essay topic, and for your ability to apply general knowledge of a specific principle or concept to a particular situation.

2 *Effective use of sources.* Tutors look for evidence in assignments of selective, relevant, and critical reading on the set essay topic. You should, therefore, find, read, evaluate, and select reliable sources that support points made by you in the assignment. The recommended reading list is the obvious place to start, but tutors often look for evidence that you have gone beyond these in your search for a range of perspectives on a subject. One tutor wrote to me to emphasize this point: 'I award 70+ marks when work demonstrates

insight and creativity in using material, including bringing material together from various parts of a course; when work shows reading outside of the course lists; and when arguments are presented in a coherent manner with examples, research evidence and a good structure'.

3 *Reasoned argument.* Tutors respect students who take an objective stance and who present valid points of view or interpretations supported with reliable **evidence** (e.g. from articles, books, statistics). The more advanced your level of study, for example, final year undergraduate or Master's, the greater should be the depth of your investigation, interpretation, analysis, and connection between subjects.

4 *A concern with matters of presentation.* Tutors expect that you will take pride in the way you present your essay. It should look good, in other words, it should be word-processed, and be free of spelling mistakes and grammatical errors. It should be written in a style that conforms with tutor expectations of academic writing on your course. Generally this means a formal, precise, and carefully written presentation. The essay should also be well structured: with a clear introduction, a logical development of ideas, and a conclusion. It should also be correctly referenced.

2.3.2 The structure of successful assignments

Hilsdon (1999) looked at the structure of successful assignments. This suggested that there are three key parts to an assignment for tutors (see diagram on page 23; adapted from Hilsdon 1999):

These stages of assignment writing will be discussed again in Chapter 5.

Main points from this chapter:

- The importance of wide reading in preparation for writing an assignment.
- The importance of answering or engaging with the set question or topic.
- The importance of using evidence to demonstrate your understanding of a subject.
- The importance of organizing your writing into a clear, coherent, and appropriate structure.
- The importance of knowing and responding to the marking criteria being used by tutors.

Introduction

Outlines what will be discussed in the assignment; puts the topic into a relevant context, e.g. states why the topic is important enough to be discussed and analysed.

Main body (includes one or more of the following)

Describes and analyses topic; demonstrates understanding of main theories, methods, ideas, or practices; illustrates how theories, ideas, methods, and practices can be applied; makes connections between ideas; understands, resolves, or deals with the situation or phenomena being discussed in the assignment.

Conclusion

Pulls ideas together; restates key learning points; may make recommendations, if a report.

3

'You have not answered or addressed the question'

Key words, propositions, and assumptions • Spot the proposition • Do you agree with the proposition? • What else? • The importance of good introductions • Keep focused on the assignment topic

---

This chapter is about:

- The value of 'unpicking' essay titles.
- The differences between descriptive and analytical assignments.
- The importance of your assignment starting well.

Have you ever received feedback on your assignment to the effect that you have 'not answered the question' or 'not engaged with the set task'? Tutors may also write, 'You did not specifically or clearly enough address the question set'. This is quite a common criticism and a main reason that tutors give as to why students fail or do badly in assignments. One tutor wrote to me on this:

> The most important thing is that students read the question before starting to write. Many students seem to just write down whatever comes to their mind with regard to a specific issue without answering the question.

If what they write doesn't contribute to answering the specific question they won't get any marks for that. It also may cause the reader to think that they don't understand the question/subject.

A tutor in another institution said much the same thing: 'I do insist on the question that I asked being answered. People are more likely to fail or do badly if they just write everything they know about a topic and don't focus on the question' (tutor quoted in Norton et al. 2007: 40).

Tutors often comment that many students tell them a lot about the subject in general, but that they do not relate this knowledge specifically or clearly enough to the assignment question or task. In other words, they haven't applied their general knowledge of a subject to the **specific** task set. Why does this happen? In some instances it is because the student assumes he or she knows a great deal about the subject generally and wants to commit enough of this knowledge onto paper – in the hope that it will convince the tutor of their reading and understanding:

> Students struggle with addressing the question sometimes, because, whether it's in the coursework or in exams, they want to tell you what they know. If they feel confident with the bit that they know about, so as long as it has some vague relationship to what you've asked, then they're going to tell you all about it (tutor quoted in Norton et al. 2007: 50).

However, a colleague wrote to me to offer a different and interesting insight:

> A number of students have told me that they feel genuinely scared of doing this kind of activity in case they find out that they can't answer the question or that they 'don't know enough'. Instead, they start with a vague idea of the topic to be addressed and plunge into the library catalogue or Google, rather than thinking about formulating an answer to a specific question. They then end up overwhelmed with information and with no yardstick against which to measure its relevance or usefulness.

So, if you have received this type of feedback, the difficulties are likely to have started at the planning stage for the assignment. The most important thing to do is to analyse the assignment task or question in detail, and make sure you are clear on what you have to do and what is expected of you. The remainder of this chapter looks at ways you can do this.

3.1 Key words, propositions, and assumptions

Successful students are those who have learned the importance of a close reading of the assignment task or question: 'The best way is to break the question down into parts and try to think, "What do they want me to say here? Which angle do I attack this question from?" And then set about strictly sticking to that plan and not wavering away from it' (student quoted in Norton et al. 2007: 48). As this student has suggested, the first thing is to be clear about what is expected of you by close reading of the assignment task title. If in doubt, you need to clarify with the tutor what approach to take. In the task title there will undoubtedly be **key words**, and there may also be **propositions** and/or **assumptions** to watch out for.

Key words are usually the ones that ask you to do something, raise the main issues, or are the main subject of the sentence. These are the words that you will almost inevitably need to define or specifically address in your assignment, to demonstrate your understanding of them and the issues they raise. Look out for the word 'and' between subject words, as this means you have to write about **both** items linked by 'and'.

Not all assignment questions contain **propositions** and/or **assumptions**, but you do need to be alert for them as they can be easily missed. Failing to address them in your assignment is a common cause of the 'not answering the question' type criticism. Propositions or assumptions often quietly propose or suggest something to you.

Propositions	Assumptions
A proposition is a definite point of view or statement that is presented for discussion. This may be in the form of a direct statement, or it may indirectly underpin the statement in question.	An assumption is a point of view that is taken for granted without the need for evidence or even discussion of the issue.

Exercise

Look at this example of an assignment task. Write in the grid below the key words and the proposition within the sentence.

Evaluate the impact of the Internet on practices for recruitment and selection employed by firms.

Identify the key words in the sentence	Spot the proposition in the sentence

3.1.1 Key words

Assuming you understand what the Internet is, the key words are:

'evaluate', 'impact', 'recruitment', 'selection', and 'firms'.

The question asks you particularly to **evaluate** (which means to weigh up or decide the importance of something) the **impact** (a significant effect) of the Internet on both recruitment **and** selection practices.

The word 'and' is quite significant, as it suggests there are two separate processes here: the recruitment process **and** the selection process. You need to be clear about each of these two separate processes. This would help to steer your assignment research – to look for evidence of the impact of the Internet, negative and positive, on both these processes. You would also need to define these terms to show you understand what is meant by them.

The term '**firms**' is plural, meaning that you need to look at more than one organization to make comparisons of some sort, perhaps between firms of different sizes.

3.1.2 What type of question or task is it?

As we have seen, one of the key words is 'evaluate'. This is a command word that defines the task, as it requires you to do something specific with the statement – in this case to assess the importance of the Internet to the recruitment and selection processes. 'Evaluate' is a typical command word found in assignment questions and task sentences. These command words can be broken into two main types:

- Descriptive.
- Analytical.

Descriptive	Analytical
Descriptive assignment questions or tasks test your knowledge of a subject and your ability to present your ideas in a clear and organised way. You are expected to identify the component parts, main elements, and distinguishing features of any topic under discussion. Descriptive command words typically include:	**Analytical** questions or tasks also test your knowledge of a subject – but they are more concerned with your ability to get below the surface of a subject and to examine it from different perspectives and points of view, and if applicable to propose alternative ideas, models, and practices. The command words for analytical questions typically include:
• Account for • Classify • Define • Demonstrate • Describe • Explain	• Analyse • Comment on • Compare and contrast • Consider • Criticize

Cont . . .

Cont . . .

Descriptive	Analytical
• Illustrate • Identify • Outline • Show how • State • Summarize • Trace	• Discuss • Distinguish between • Evaluate • Examine • Explore • Interpret • Justify

It is possible to group these command terms into common meaning and action prompts, as follows:

Descriptive terms	Action expected
• Define • Describe • State • Classify • Identify	You are expected to locate, identify, and present the **main features**, elements, or components of the topic under discussion and, if applicable, the underpinning theoretical knowledge of the subject.
• Demonstrate • Illustrate • Show how	As above, plus you would be expected to present and explain **examples** to show that you understand how something works, e.g. how a theory, model, idea, or practice can be applied to a given situation.
• Outline • Summarize	You are expected to identify and summarize the main points of the topic under discussion.
• Trace	This means that you identify and outline the stages of development of the topic under discussion.
• Account for • Explain	You would clarify why something is as it is, or what happened in any given situation.
Analytical terms	Action expected
• Discuss • Examine • Explore • Evaluate • Consider • Interpret • Comment on	If you see any of these command terms you are expected to identify and explain the main features of the subject under discussion, including the main theories, ideas, models, or practices underpinning the topic. If applicable, you would be expected to know of and weigh up any counter-arguments and to make connections between different ideas, models, or practices.

Analytical terms	Action expected
• Analyse • Criticize	This involves a **detailed scrutiny** of the topic in question. This could include explaining the origins, structure, organization, or development of the topic in question, the positive and negative features of it, and the connections between theories, ideas, models, and practices. You would also demonstrate your awareness of any flaws in particular points of view, and your knowledge of alternative viewpoints.
• Justify	This involves making out a case and giving reasons to support a particular viewpoint, position, judgement, or decision against other possibilities.
• Compare and contrast • Distinguish between	This involves a close study of the differences between one idea, phenomena, or situation, and another. You would need to identify the structure or features of one and make comparisons with another. You may be required to make a judgement on which is more applicable or relevant for the situation in question.

You will also encounter combined questions or tasks involving both descriptive and analytical approaches. These may take the form of part (a) questions, which are often descriptive in nature, followed by part (b), which are often more analytical. Although both parts are important, tutors are likely to put more emphasis and the weighting of marks onto the analytical part of your answer.

But let us come back to the assignment title we are considering in this chapter so far:

> **Evaluate the impact of the Internet on practices for recruitment and selection employed by firms.**

In this example you are asked to 'evaluate', which requires an **analytical** approach to the subject. One way to start with this particular task is to spot the proposition within the sentence.

3.2 Spot the proposition

Earlier in this chapter I suggested that the task sentence, in addition to command sentences, also presented you with a proposition, although this may have been harder to detect. It proposes that the Internet **has** had an impact on recruitment and selection; it stresses the words 'the impact', which suggests there **has** been one.

3.3 Do you agree with the proposition?

So you are being asked to think about whether or not you agree that this proposition is correct – and you don't **have** to agree with the proposition. For example, if you disagreed with the proposition, you could argue that the Internet has had little or no impact on recruitment and selection – assuming you could find evidence to support this position. The point is that assignment tasks, particularly essays, are often quite provocative; they prod you to take up a position and to support it with reliable evidence. There may not be, and probably will not be, a 'right' answer to essay questions of this type. Tutors are testing your ability to research and weigh up evidence, take up a considered position, and present a point of view in an intelligent and coherent way. They may not agree with the position you take, but will certainly respect your ability to argue your case in an intelligent way.

The two main positions that you would take in this essay on the Internet, for example, are:

Agree generally	Disagree generally
Agreeing with the proposition and presenting evidence and summarising why you agree.	**Disagreeing** that there has been an 'impact', or that it has been very limited, and presenting evidence and discussing why you feel this to be the case.

You begin to 'evaluate' when you start to adopt a position, as you are making a decision on the proposition and, in this case, assessing the importance of the Internet to the recruitment and selection processes.

3.4 What else?

If you are evaluating the impact of the Internet, you would also need to weigh up the value (if any) of the Internet against non-electronic ways of engaging with the recruitment and selection processes.

So, how do you make sure you answer the question or engage with the set task in this particular Internet question example?

What you should do to engage with the set task

- Write a **clear introduction** explaining to the reader what you are going to discuss (see example later in this chapter).

Descriptive features:

- Outline the range of methods open to employers for staff recruitment and selection purposes, including the Internet.
- Present detail on the nature and impact of the Internet generally in recent years, and describe how the Internet is currently used for both recruitment and selection purposes by both employers and jobseekers (jobseekers can use the Internet to their advantage too, to seek for vacancies).

Analytical features:

- Give advantages of the Internet for both recruitment and selection purposes.
- Show you understand the disadvantages of the Internet for both recruitment and selection purposes.
- Make comparison with non-electronic methods of recruitment and selection.
- Conclusion: pull your ideas together and reach a conclusion.

3.5 The importance of good introductions

As stated earlier in Chapter 2, an effective introduction is a vital element in overcoming criticism that you 'failed to answer the question'. The concept of 'positive reinforcement' is worth mentioning here. When a tutor looks at your assignment the first thing they read is the introduction. This creates an impression of you. If the introduction is good, a positive impression is generated of you, which will influence how your tutor approaches the remainder of your assignment. In other words, they will seek for reinforcement of their first good impression of you in the remainder of your work.

Unfortunately the converse can also apply. If you start badly, this creates a negative impression, and this may lead to a situation where other badly written parts of the assignment reinforce the negative impression created. Tutors try hard to overcome this bias. But as long as humans and not androids are still marking assignments, this situation is somewhat inevitable. So your introduction needs to be as good as you can make it. But what makes a good introduction?

Example

Here is an example of an introduction for this assignment title:

> The Internet has had a significant impact worldwide on recruitment practices within organisations of all sizes. In the area of selection, advances have been slower, but there have been some interesting online selection initiatives. These include automated filtering of applications, initial psychological testing of applicants, and networking systems for interviewing and selecting candidates. This essay will attempt to describe and evaluate the impact the Internet has had on both these two aspects of human resources management.

Think about what is 'happening' in this introduction. Remember, the assignment task was to:

Evaluate the impact of the Internet on practices for recruitment and selection employed by firms.

The introduction example for this assignment:

- Immediately engages with the proposition (agrees with it) in relation to one of the two practices (recruitment): 'The Internet has had a significant impact world-wide on recruitment practices within organisations of all sizes'.
- But is more cautious about the selection stage: 'In the area of selection, advances have been slower, but there are, nevertheless, some interesting on-line selection initiatives'.
- By doing this the student shows that he or she has identified the need to deal with both the process of recruitment **and** selection.
- Note too, the repeating of the word 'impact', taken from the task title, which thereby shows the tutor the title has been read and understood. The student also puts the impact into a geographical context, i.e. 'worldwide'.
- Some brief examples are presented, thereby demonstrating immediately to the tutor that the student can identify and relate specific practice to the selection process generally: 'These include automated filtering of applications, initial psychological testing of applicants, and networking systems for interviewing and selecting candidates'.
- The student also states what briefly what he or she intends to do; note again the repetition of a word from the title, 'evaluate', thus showing the tutor that the task is understood, and that evaluation is a separate intellectual process from 'describe'. The student again reminds the tutor that both processes of recruitment **and** selection will be discussed: 'This essay will attempt to describe and evaluate the impact the Internet has had on both these two aspects of human resources management'.

This form of introduction is a sound and reliable way of getting started, but not the only way. Other examples of effective introductions are presented in Chapter 5.

3.6 Keep focused on the assignment topic

Once you start to write, it is important you do not deviate from the assignment topic or question. A number of experienced tutors have collectively offered this advice: 'A tip is to look at every single paragraph you write and ask yourself "Is this paragraph answering the question?" If the answer is "yes", leave it in, if "no", get rid of it!' (Quoted in Norton et al. 2007: 39).

Exercise

Look at the following assignment questions or tasks taken from a range of disciplines. Try at least one of these and identify the key words and any assumptions or propositions (if any) in the statements. Then try and summarize what is expected of you. Clearly the **depth** of engagement with the tasks will depend on what stage of undergraduate or postgraduate study you are at. But there would be broad expectations of all students in terms of how they would tackle the subject and the approach and direction they would take to the task. Use the spaces provided for your answers. When you have finished look at Appendix 2 in this book for comments.

Example 1

It can be said that the longstanding nature–nurture argument about the development of human behaviour still rages today. Some theorists take the position that behaviour is attributable to genetic factors, while others argue that environmental factors are responsible. Explore this issue, with reference to relevant theorists and commentators.

Key words	Any propositions or assumptions?	What's expected of you

Example 2

> What is the difference between a conductor and an insulator? Give experimental evidence for the descriptions that you give, and try to account for these descriptions using a microscopic model of the material.

Key words	Any propositions or assumptions?	What's expected of you

Example 3

> 'History is more or less bunk. It's tradition. We don't want tradition. We want to live in the present, and the only history that is worth a tinker's damn is the history that we make today.' (Henry Ford 1916). Discuss.

Key words	Any propositions or assumptions?	What's expected of you

Example 4

Evaluate the concerns that for all the talk of a new flexible workforce the reality is somewhat more contradictory and problematic.

Key words	Any propositions or assumptions?	What's expected of you

Look at Appendix 2 for comments.

Main points from this chapter:

- The way to avoid criticism that 'you have not answered or addressed the question' is to analyse the task question or statement. This means identifying **key words** and focusing on **command words**, which define the approach you need to adopt.
- You should also identify **propositions** or **assumptions** (although not all questions or task statements will have these).
- A clear introduction that signposts the reader to what you have to say is essential (see also Chapter 5).
- Identify and present evidence to support the position you have adopted.
- Keep focused on the assignment task; don't deviate, no matter how tempting this can be.

4

'Your work is more descriptive than critical'

Critical thinking/critical analysis • Six ways to be analytical • Getting started • Analysing theories • Six ways to question a theory (or idea, model, or practice) • The Janus face of arguments • Identifying flaws in arguments • Constructing your own arguments

This chapter is about:

- What is meant by the terms 'critical analysis' or 'critical thinking'.
- Ways of becoming more analytical in assignments.
- Identifying flaws in arguments.

Tutors may present a variation on the same theme in their feedback comments. They might say, for example: 'Your assignment did not explore the subject in enough depth'; or 'You should have analysed the subject more thoroughly'; or that there was 'too much description (or narration) and not enough analysis'; or 'You did not apply much critical thinking to this topic'. One tutor is reported to have commented metaphorically to a student: 'analytically, it is rather undernourished' (quoted by Channock 2000: 96).

This chapter will explain, therefore, what is meant by 'critical analysis' and 'critical thinking', and will present you with some ways of moving beyond description toward analysis in assignments – but only when that is needed and necessary.

4.1 Critical thinking/critical analysis

To start with do not be intimidated by the terms 'critical thinking' and 'critical analysis'. They sound daunting, but at the heart of the whole process is the very human instinct to be curious and to seek answers to questions. You could replace the terms 'critical analysis/thinking' with 'ways of asking questions', and you would have cracked the code! If you are someone who does not take things for granted and are a natural sceptic when faced with 'expert' opinion, you are well on your way to developing your aptitude for critical thinking in assignments. You should keep in mind the comments of Colin Powell, Chairman of the US Joint Chiefs of Staff, during 1989–93: 'Don't be buffaloed by experts and elites. Experts often possess more data than judgement' (Powell 2007).

However, this scepticism and questioning of authority comes more easily to some students than to others, and some international students, for example, can experience difficulty at first with the whole notion of critical analysis. In the West, as mentioned in Chapter 2, the education system rewards students with high marks for analytical or creative expressions of ideas in assignments; but this may not always be the case in other countries where there are other criteria for assessing student knowledge.

This form of independent critical thinking may be unfamiliar to students from overseas, for example, who in the past have been rewarded by their tutors for presenting accurate description of established ideas. The prospect of challenging the say-so of 'experts' can, at first, feel daunting, and even subversive.

The prospect of deconstructing and commenting on academic arguments in an essay, rather than simply acknowledging and restating them is a genuinely fearful one [for many international students], despite the obvious desire of these students to want to get things 'right' and go home with the qualification they came here to get (Johnson 2007).

A Chinese colleague wrote to me on this issue:

British people are brought up to think critically – this can initially be quite shocking to other cultures. In the Far East, students are encouraged to learn by imitation. But within three months, these students get used to this and settle in very well – it quickly becomes quite exciting!

4.2 Six ways to be analytical

Critical analysis is about looking at a subject from a range of perspectives, following or creating logical points of view (or 'arguments'), and looking for your own direction to take in assignments. There is at least one of six directions you could take:

1 **Agreeing** with a particular point of view, but presenting reliable evidence to support the position taken.
2 **Rejecting** a particular point of view, but again using reliable evidence to do this.
3 **Conceding** that an existing point of view has merits, but that it needs to be qualified in certain respects, and stating what these are.
4 **Proposing** a new point of view, or reformulating an existing one, backed with supporting evidence.
5 **Reconciling** two positions, which may seem at variance, by bringing a new perspective to bear on the topic.
6 **Connecting or synthesizing** different ideas, so that new approaches and points of view can be advanced.

(Adapted from Taylor 1989)

In addition to the 'six ways to be analytical', it can be argued that **detailed description** is a way too of engaging analytically with some assignment tasks. This can involve focusing on a topic in a detailed way. In many science and technology disciplines, for example, this focus can include the observation and identification of variables, element parts, and structures. In this context, the analysis is in the detailed description that you present. You are likely to be asked in these assignments to:

* Classify.
* Describe.
* Identify.
* Show how.
* Or answer 'what' or 'how' style questions.

Example: an assignment title requiring a detailed descriptive analysis

> Throughout history, technological developments have enabled artists and architects to express ideas in new ways. Choose and fully identify and describe two works of art or architecture that connect with this view and the specific technological developments that made each work possible.

It is true to say, however, that the assignments presenting students with the greatest difficulties are often those that start with description or definition, but then require students to move outwards by seeking answers to the 'what' and 'why' range of questions in order to explain phenomena and situations. The difficulties are often about selecting which information to include in assignments – and which to leave out. Some topics are 'large', in the sense that so much can be said – but you have only two or three thousand words to say it. Here are two such examples:

Examples: assignment titles with 'large' topic areas

1 'Identify the driving forces of globalization today and discuss their impact.'
2 ' "The individual is free to make choices, and any outcomes can be explained exclusively through the study of his or her ideas and decisions". Discuss.'

4.3 Getting started

When faced with a 'big' topic area, similar to the examples given above, and with a restricted word limit, one's first instinct is to freeze mentally. Where do you start?

The way forward is to make preliminary notes that:

1 Identify any key words.
2 Identify any assumptions or propositions in the title – which you will need to address in your assignment.
3 Highlight what you know already about it, to identify what additional research and reading you need to do.

The first two of these, *1* and *2*, as discussed in Chapter 3, will help you to focus on the assignment title, and the third, *3*, will help you to explore the subject in an analytical way.

The following are examples of preliminary notes.

Example: Preliminary notes for title (1) – 'Identify the driving forces of globalization today and discuss their impact.'

> Key words: 'identify' (pick out); 'driving forces' and 'globalisation' (explain); 'today' – deliberate inclusion of word suggests a comparison between 'globalization' in the past and present; 'discuss their impact': identify and weigh up consequences – mixture of positive and negative.
>
> Propositions/assumptions: task assumes that all driving forces can be 'identified'. I need to check this out – see what commentators have to say about this; there may be 'hidden' forces?
>
> Notes: Need to define globalization – not new – how does it differ today from the past? What makes it different today? Driving forces: Speed of communication – Internet; political changes: demise of communism; expansion of trade; development of global institutions: the World Trade Organisation; the International Monetary Fund; the World Bank; etc.
>
> Impact: faster communication; spread of knowledge; increased trade and lessening of hostility between nations, compared with recent past. But four big issues: Monopolisation of Trade by Multinational Organisations; Global Inequality; Environmental Issues; Cultural Changes and tensions.
>
> Need to check out: read more about 'alternatives to globalization' ideas: can/should impact of global institutions be lessened?

The student is at a fairly advanced state of preparing to write the assignment, but needs to engage with some additional reading.

Example: Preliminary notes for title (2) – ' "The individual is free to make choices, and any outcomes can be explained exclusively through the study of his or her ideas and decisions." Discuss.'

> Key words: 'Individual' (define; individual also a part of a collective); 'free' (what's 'free'? How 'free'?) and 'can be explained exclusively' – meaning 'just by'; 'study' (close examination); 'ideas and decisions' (meaning: cognition and action).
>
> Propositions: 'is free'; 'can be explained' 'exclusively'. I need to take up a position: agree; disagree; partly agree/disagree?
>
> Notes: class and reading notes that seem relevant: determinism; self-determinism; free will; I could use my experience of writing this assign-ment as a way of illustrating theories: I have to 'decide' on a position to take in the essay (self-determinism?) But I am influenced by determinism: I make choices, Ok, but are these really 'free' ones – I'm influenced by external factors and needs of others! 'Soft-determinism'?
>
> Read again: James article: Dilemma of Determinism; go over course notes again.

This student is apparently at an early stage of preparation for writing the assignment, but has identified the main issues that need to be explored and clarified. Most importantly, the student has identified the propositions in the title and the need to address these.

4.4 Analysing theories

Analysing theoretical ideas or models is an important part of critical analysis. How do you move from description of a theory to a critical analysis of it? Try this exercise.

Exercise

The following is an extract from a student assignment on the management of change. The student presents a description of William Bridges' four-stage theory of individual change. However, critical thinking is often about **evaluating or analysing** ideas like this. What questions might the student have posed or asked to begin to challenge the theory?

As you read the extract, imagine you had William Bridges sitting next to you. What questions would you like to ask him to clarify or explain his ideas to you? Write your questions in the space below the extract.

William Bridges (1980) discusses the process of individual change by presenting four stages: disengagement, 'disidentification', disorientation and disenchantment that individuals must pass through to move into the transition state and effectively change.

The first stage of **disengagement** involves breaking with the old organizational practices and behaviours. Typical human responses exhibited will be refusal to engage with the change process, running away, quitting, seeking a transfer or taking early retirement, absenteeism and withdrawal of interest. After making the break, individuals need to be more flexible and recognize that they are not who they were before.

This is the second stage of **'disidentification'** in which individuals tend to hang onto the past and have a distorted view of the future. This takes place when the individual's values and something he identifies with are removed e.g. specific tasks, location, team, expertise and there seems to be nothing equivalent to replace it.

Disenchantment is the third stage of individual change in which individuals further clear away the 'old,' challenge assumptions and create a deeper sense of reality for themselves by recognising that what once was is no more, something which they once valued has been taken away. Disenchantment is often associated with anger which is easier to deal with when expressed directly and if suppressed may come out in more indirect ways.

In the fourth stage of individual change, **disorientation**, individuals feel lost and confused. This is a very necessary but unpleasant state as individuals move into the transition state and to a new beginning. Disoriented people lose sight of where they fit in and what they should be doing and have trouble making sense of the new order of things.

The reactions to change described above are typical human responses during uncertainty and change.

What questions would you want to ask Bridges about his four stage idea? Write in the space that follows:

Questions you would want to ask William Bridges

Look at Appendix 3 for comments on this exercise.

4.5 Six ways to question a theory (or idea, model, or practice)

There are six main ways to 'question a theory'. You can ask questions about:

1 Methodology.
2 Applicability.
3 Exceptions to the rule.
4 The cultural adaptability of the theory.
5 Its contemporary 'currency' (is it still valid today?).
6 Its relevance to you and your own experiences.

You can use these questions in a worksheet format, similar to the one shown next, to remind yourself of the questions to ask.

Methodology • How did the author(s) of the ideas arrive at their conclusions? • Was it on the basis of research using primary data, or based on their own personal experiences? • What methods and sample were used to gather data or test the ideas? Do these appear reliable? • Has the research been tested by others using similar methodology? If so, what was the result?	
Applicability • How can or could the theory be applied? • Has the theory been applied? If so, when, where, how, and with what result? • What are the main counter-arguments to the theory generally, or in relation to particular situations?	
Exceptions • What are the 'exceptions to the rule' in relation to the theory – and why? • Which situations or contexts do **not** connect with the theory – and why? • Could the theory adapt or change to suit the situation in question? If so, how, when, where, and in what way?	
Cultural adaptability **We live in a world that transmits ideas quickly, so . . .** • To what extent, if at all, does the theory adapt to other societies and cultures? • Is it only applicable in a particular cultural context? • And if 'yes' to the above question, **why** does culture have an impact on the applicability of the idea in question?	
Currency • Was the idea a product or a result of a particular period in history – if so why? • How valid is the idea today? • Have the original author(s) updated their ideas since original publication?	
Does it make sense to you? • Does the idea make sense to you from your own experiences? **This can be a good starting point for exploring ideas. However, If the idea does** connect with your experiences, keep open to counter-arguments and be willing to change your mind.	

4.6 The Janus face of arguments

Janus was the Roman God of gates and doors, and was represented with a double-faced head, with the faces looking in opposite directions. The idea of a gateway, and opposite directions, as an analogy for 'argument' can be a useful way of thinking about this issue. Building a strong argument is an important part of gaining access to an assignment and choosing which direction to go.

The term 'argument' in this case does not mean having an angry altercation with someone. It means building a strong case to support a particular position, rather like an advocate does in court. And rather like the advocate, the more objective and calm you appear when you present your case, the stronger your case can appear to be. Your arguments in an assignment will consist of the individual points you make, which lead to the overall conclusions you reach.

Often the assignments that gain the best marks are those where students demonstrate that they understand the arguments both for and against a particular point of view, but then put forward their own conclusions, or summarize the perspectives they find the most persuasive.

However, you need to be alert to some of the main pitfalls in arguments.

4.7 Identifying flaws in arguments

A key component in critical thinking is about identifying flaws in arguments. Here are four common flaws:

- Assuming an invalid causal link.
- False or spurious correlations.
- Gaps in arguments.
- False analogies.

1 *Assuming an invalid causal link.* This is when two things are found together and an **invalid assumption** is made that there must be a connection or link between them.

Examples

> Boadicea had red hair, which contributed to her fiery and warlike nature.
>
> The counsel for the defence claimed that his client's constant exposure to TV crime shows was responsible for '. . . moulding his behaviour in a twisted way. Without the influence of television . . . there would not have been any crime'

2 *False or spurious correlations*. When trends or phenomena are shown to be related this is referred to as correlation. A **correlation** shows some reliable mutual relationship or association between variables; for example: 'As the temperature lowers, people wear more layers of clothes'.

However, if a correlation is assumed where none exists, this is a *false correlation*. It is about assuming that if B follows A, then A has caused B. For example: 'Research has been shown that beer drinkers obtain lower grades at assignments than non-beer drinkers'.

In this example, an unwarranted assumption is being made that, since beer drinking and low grades go together, beer drinking **causes** low grades. However, in this case it is possible that B precedes A: it could be that it is the low grades that cause people to drink beer!

3 *Mind the gap*. Critical analysis for academic purposes often involves asking, 'Is anything missing from this argument?' It can be tempting for authors to conveniently forget to include evidence that may not completely endorse, or that may even contradict, the overall point they are making. When analysing ideas you need to look at all the elements and components and, in particular, ask yourself, 'Are all the relevant elements being considered?' The essential question to ask when examining an argument is, 'Has anything been left out of the equation?'

4 *Analogy and false analogy*. An analogy is a comparison made to draw out similarities between two things. It will express a correspondence, equivalence, or parallel alignment between two things because of some element that they share, for example, 'January is to winter, as October is to autumn'. Creative writing often involves making imaginative and unusual comparisons, often through similes, or metaphors, for example, 'The silence echoed between them and roared their mutual dislike'. However, for most academic writing you would normally use more valid and prosaic comparisons, for example, the heart works as a pump, moving blood through the body by opening and constricting. The comparison with a pump is a **valid comparison** (or analogy).

However, an **invalid comparison** is when:

- The two items being compared are not sufficiently similar;

- The comparison is misleading; or
- The item used for comparison is described inaccurately.

The analogy is not valid (**a false analogy**) if it does not compare like with like.

Example

> A college is not so different from a business. It needs a clear, competitive strategy that will lead to profitable growth.

In this example, the values of both sets of organizations are different, which can affect the outcomes and the processes within them – although there may be similarities in the ways people in both are managed.

4.8 Constructing your own arguments

To help you develop your own argument, you could use a grid similar to the one that follows to help you focus on and clarify both sides of a particular argument/idea/point of view. You can then summarize the overall position you will take in the assignment.

So one of the main ways of avoiding feedback comments that your work is more descriptive than analytical is to make sure you show your tutor that you understand different points of view on a topic and, after weighing up the arguments, you state your own considered position.

Main points from this chapter:

- At the heart of critical thinking and analysis is asking questions and not taking anything for granted.
- Critical thinking and analysis can also involve a close scrutiny and accurate description of something.
- An 'argument' in academic terms is about building a strong case to support a particular position taken in an assignment.
- It is important to be aware of the main flaws in arguments so you avoid them yourselves – and can spot them in other people's work.

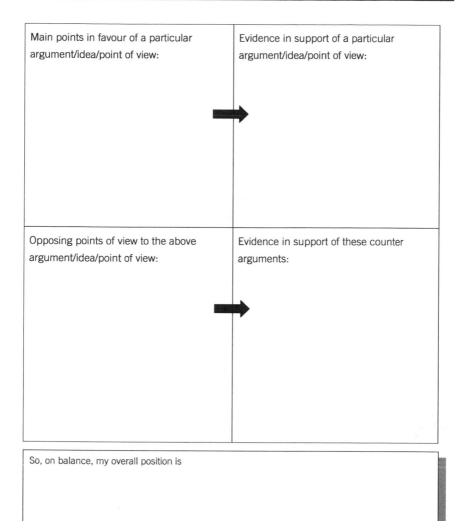

Main points in favour of a particular argument/idea/point of view:

Evidence in support of a particular argument/idea/point of view:

Opposing points of view to the above argument/idea/point of view:

Evidence in support of these counter arguments:

So, on balance, my overall position is

5

'Your assignment was poorly structured'

Essays • Introductions • Conclusions • Report structure

This chapter is about:

- Organizing essays and reports.
- The importance of good introductions and conclusions.
- Making your ideas cascade and connect with each other.

Students often say they have read up on the subject and ideas are buzzing round in their head, but that they have problems organizing their thoughts and expressing what they know in a coherent way. If this applies to you, and you have been receiving feedback from tutors to this effect, then this chapter will help you begin to organize and structure your work more effectively. 'Structure' essentially means the way the assignment has been pieced together and presented to any reader, rather like a pleasing jigsaw puzzle. The structure of both essays and reports will be discussed, and the chapter will also include examples of both a short essay and a report to illustrate the points made.

5.1 Essays

You may remember that Chapter 2 outlined the essential differences between writing essays and reports. In summary, an effective essay structure will broadly take this shape:

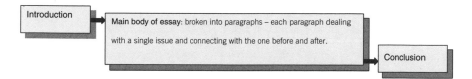

Sounds easy, doesn't it? But if you struggle with the whole notion of structuring your work you will know that it is not at all easy. However, you may find the following approach helpful in planning and structuring your ideas before you start writing the assignment.

You can do this in a series of stages or steps. This chapter contain a worksheet that can be used when planning an essay, but you can easily design your own for future use.

5.1.1 Step one: the essay title

The important thing, as emphasized in Chapters 3 and 4, is to think about what issues are raised by the assignment title. Note that, at this stage, you are looking at the **title** only. This is important, as understanding the title will help you to steer the assignment in the right direction and keep you focused on this.

As stated earlier:

- You might, for example, pick out some key words in the title and think about the wider issues raised by them.
- You might want to clarify or question the ideas or assumptions behind the words used in the title.
- You may also want to challenge or explore the whole proposition of the assignment question or task.

Before you start to write your essay, you need to **brainstorm** all the issues that come up to the surface for you in the **title**. Use the box that follows to brainstorm the issues that flow from the title.

Exercise

(Write out your assignment question or task in full in the space below).

Look closely at the words in the title. Pick out key words; highlight any assumptions or propositions; look out for command words: what are you being asked to do? Write down anything that occurs to you about the title.

Key words	Any propositions or assumptions?	What's expected of you

5.1.2 Step two: the essay subject

Having clarified your response to the essay title, the next step involves brain-storming the essay **subject or topic** itself. This will involve you bringing to the surface ideas, arguments, sources, points of view, and opinions that are relevant to the topic, and identifying the direction set by the title. You just need to jot these down as they occur to you. This stage of the process assumes, of course, you have done some reading on the subject in question!

Exercise

Use the space that follows for your brainstorming of the essay subject/topic.

5.1.3 Step three: decide on your point of view

Having brainstormed the title and the subject, in some essays you will need to decide what is going to be your position, main argument, view or perspective in the essay. **This is particularly important in analytical essays** (see Chapters 3 and 4) as it is all too easy to write an essay that gives a range of perspectives, but still leaves the reader puzzled as to **your** conclusions or position. **Your** point of view is important, but it needs to be backed up with valid evidence.

If the essay is implicitly or explicitly seeking you to take up a position, what is it going to be? What will be your overall point of view?

Exercise

In the space below, write a 'mini-essay' in 50 words that neatly summarizes your point of view for the assignment.

5.1.4 Step four: subdivide your ideas into separate paragraphs

The next stage of the process involves sorting out your ideas into a readable and coherent form. You should aim to make your ideas 'flow' and connect, and you need to group your ideas into paragraphs.

There is no set length for a paragraph, although it would be unusual for one to be over three-quarters of a page. Think carefully also about the use of two or three line paragraphs, as these can be irritating for some readers. The paragraph should contain one, or at the most, two **key idea** sentences. These are often found at the start of each paragraph, and the remaining sentences will develop this key idea. A common mistake in essay writing is to hop around from one unrelated idea to another. So, you need to decide on what main point you are going to make in each paragraph – and stick to this.

Example: a paragraph taken from an essay on distance learning for managers

> Distance learning has a number of advantages for the busy manager. It can, almost always, give managers control of their learning. Unlike traditionally taught, face-to-face learners, distance learners are free to choose when and where they study. If managers are up to their necks in budget forecasts or resolving crises during one particular week, then, as long as they make up the time the next week, their study time does not have to suffer. Study can be fitted in and around the demands of a busy work schedule and, essentially, distance learners do not have to give up their jobs whilst they are studying. Unlike their counterparts who are taught face-to-face, distance-taught managers can usually relate what they study to their immediate work situation as they are learning. They can read about a management concept and then see if it makes sense at their place of work the very next day. Similarly, research in the workplace can be easily undertaken in support of course work and assignments, and constant exchanges of theory and practice are facilitated. Also, at the end of their studies, the distance-taught managers simply carry on working, whereas their colleagues who have been taught face-to-face may have to pick up the threads after a prolonged period of absence (Giles and Hedge 1998: 57).

In the paragraph above the **key idea** sentence is the first one: 'Distance learning has a number of advantages for the busy manager'; the other sentences build on this key idea.

You can now start to fit your ideas together – one idea per paragraph.

Exercise

The boxes that follow will help you do this. Think of one box as containing one idea and representing a paragraph in your essay. Look back at your brain-storming ideas around the essay subject or topic. Think about how you can unscramble these and arrange them into the boxes: **one box** = one topic idea or element of description only. In each box write one main heading or brief sentence to summarize the point you wish to make. Use more boxes if you wish:

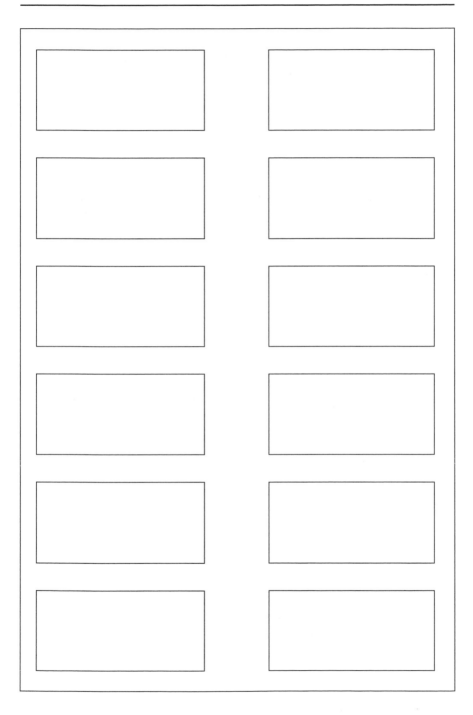

5.1.5 Step five: connecting your ideas

- The next stage is to try and arrange these paragraphs into a structure or sequence that 'flows', so that one paragraph (and key idea) connects logically with the next.
- You can number the boxes 1, 2, 3, and so on, in the sequence you intend those ideas to appear in your essay.
- There should be a sense of progression: you introduce your assignment to the reader, introduce your ideas, develop your ideas, and reach a conclusion.

There is no set formula for structuring an essay. The important thing about good essay structure is about making logical connections from one paragraph to the next. If you have a rough shape and plan to your writing at the start, this will serve as a guide through the mist, and it is likely that the shape will clarify further as you begin to write and put your plan into effect.

You may find that some study skills textbooks argue that you should present one or more paragraphs presenting one view, then one or more paragraphs presenting a counterview, before arriving at a conclusion. This might work for some 'discuss' type assignments but not all assignments. There may be occasions, if you had valid and reliable evidence to support the stance, when you might want to pursue one viewpoint consistently throughout the essay. Counter-arguments, for example, can be addressed within an essay that takes and maintains one particular position throughout. Your arguments may implicitly or explicitly address these counter-arguments, which will demonstrate to your tutor your reading on the subject.

With essays that require a largely descriptive approach to a subject, you can build unified layers of description throughout the assignment until you present as complete and comprehensive a picture as possible. The aim with this type of descriptive assignment is to test your non-judgemental understanding or observation of a subject, how it connects with other phenomenon, and how theories, models, ideas, and practices can be applied to real or theoretical situations.

5.1.6 Step six: introductions and conclusions

A clear introduction to your essay is vital, as it sets the scene for the essay as a whole (see also Chapters 3 and 4). You also need a conclusion that pulls your ideas together, confirms your viewpoint, or reminds the reader of your main point(s) made.

5.2 Introductions

As emphasized earlier in this book, the opening paragraph, the introduction to the essay, is very important for three reasons:

- Gaining the reader's attention.
- Setting yourself a purpose; a clear direction and structure to the essay.
- Creating a positive impression of you in the mind of the reader, in this case, your tutor.

Two reliable ways of getting started:

1 The 'tell them what you are going to tell them' approach.
2 The 'quote a quote' approach.

Two examples from each approach follow:

5.2.1 The 'tell them what you are going to tell them' approach

Example 1

> This essay will consider the paradox of intelligence, one of the nine paradoxes that Charles Handy outlines in 'The Empty Raincoat' (1994). A central point that Handy makes in this book is the importance of encouraging adults to consider continuous learning throughout their lives. This may be an important and worthy aim, but is it feasible? This essay will explore just how realistic this aim is.
>
> The essay is structured into three main parts. In the first part the distribution of academic qualifications and social class characteristics of adults in Britain today will be examined to look at the relationship between adult continuing education and social class. Next, the impact of these social factors will be explored further, with a particular focus on why a majority of British adults appear reluctant to return to formal education or training. Finally, the issue of what might be done to encourage more adults to consider education and training as a relevant option in their lives will be discussed. A central point in this essay will be that UK government policy on financial support for adult learners needs to change in order to encourage more back to formal learning.

Example 2

It is essential for healthcare professionals to develop their skills and knowledge in order for them to provide quality services and advice, and to reduce errors. This has led to the introduction of Continual Professional Development (CPD) systems. But what impact has CPD had on service performance? This essay will review the impact of CPD in one branch of healthcare . . . [**states which**], and in particular will explore evidence concerning the understanding and views of practitioners on compulsory CPD and their perceptions of its impact on their professional practice.

5.2.2 The 'quote-a-quote' approach

Example 1

Charles Handy, in 'The Empty Raincoat' (1994), argues that we need to 'transform the whole of society into a permanent learning culture' (p.25). This essay will discuss how realistic a prospect this is in Britain today. It will be argued that, although attitudes to education are changing, there are still too many social, cultural and economic barriers for many adults to overcome before they will consider education or training as a serious option in their lives. The essay will examine how the social transformation that Handy asserts is necessary, might be achieved.

Example 2

'I don't need to ordered to continue my professional development; I do it anyway because I am a professional'. This quotation is at the core of a debate about the introduction of mandatory Continuous Professional Development (CPD) in the . . . [states which] healthcare profession. On one side of the debate are those that argue that professional responsibilities and ethics will, and should, act as a spur to professional development, and that compulsion is unnecessary; whilst on the other side are those that argue that CPD simply provides a structure for this to happen, and safeguards the profession against a very small minority who do not take their responsibilities for professional development as seriously as they might. This essay will explore both sides of this current debate.

5.3 Conclusions

The concluding paragraph will remind the reader of how you have answered or addressed the question or set task. You do not always **have** to have come to a definite position on one side or the other, because, as stated earlier, in the more descriptive style of essay your task was primarily to summarize the main theories or features of a topic. There also needs to be a definite indication and sense that you have reached the end of the essay.

Sentences you could use in your concluding paragraph to signal the end of the essay include:

- This essay has shown that . . .
- In conclusion then, the main points in this debate are these . . .
- Finally, it can be said that . . .
- The balance of arguments suggests that . . .
- Despite the evidence to the contrary, it could be argued . . .

Quotations, if relevant to the topic, can also be an excellent way of ending an essay, as they can make the reader think.

A sample essay written by an undergraduate student now follows. (If you would prefer to read an essay written by a postgraduate student, then see Chapter 10.) The essay is followed by a commentary on the structure and an exercise to consolidate your learning.

Example: a sample essay

Title:

Evaluate the impact of the Internet on practices for recruitment and selection employed by firms.

(*This sample essay has had paragraph numbers added to aid discussion. Essays would not normally have numbered paragraphs.*)

1 The Internet has had a significant global impact on recruitment practices within organisations of all sizes. In the area of selection, advances have been slower, but there are, nevertheless, some interesting on-line selection initiatives. These include automated filtering of applications, initial psychological testing of applicants, and networking systems for interviewing and selecting candidates. This essay will attempt to describe and evaluate the impact the Internet has had on both these two aspects of human resources management.

2 The Internet is a system of connecting computers around the world. Linked to this is the 'Intranet', which is a way organisations can

communicate internally. The population connected to the Internet in 1999 totalled some 196 million people, predicted to rise to over 500 million by the end of 2003. The number of worldwide Email mailboxes is expected to increase at a compound annual growth rate of 138 percent, from 505 million in 2000 to 1.2 billion in 2005 (International Data Corporation 2001).

3 The Internet has had a significant impact on the way both firms and job seekers seek each other out. In Britain in 2000, it was estimated that 47 per cent of all employers were making use of the Internet for recruitment purposes (Dale 2003). In the USA the Association of Internet Recruiters estimated that 45 per cent of companies surveyed had filled one in five of their vacancies through on-line recruiting (Charles 2000). More than 75 per cent of Human Resources personnel in the USA are now making regular use of Internet job boards, in addition to traditional recruitment methods of newspaper advertising and links with employment agencies (HR Focus 2001).

4 The main ways that firms use the Internet include developing their own websites, making use of recruitment agency sites, or using 'job boards': external websites that carry sometimes thousands of vacancies available for job seekers to scan. Increasingly, external recruitment agencies are specialising in particular types of niche vacancies, or acting as career managers for job applicants, helping to both place the applicant in the right job and support that person during their career.

5 Job seekers too, can use the Internet to contact prospective employers by placing their CVs or work résumés on to websites that employers can scan. A survey in the USA in 1999 suggested that 55 per cent of graduates had posted their résumé on to an online job service, and that three-quarters had used the Internet to search for jobs in specific geographic locations (Monday et al 2002). Some job seekers, with high demand skills, offer their labour in electronic 'talent auctions', with job negotiations, once a successful match has been made, facilitated by the Auction House representatives on behalf of the applicants.

6 The main advantages to employers of using the Internet for recruitment purposes are in the speed of operation, breadth of coverage, particularly if recruiting on a world-wide basis, and the cost saving that can occur. Electronic advertising can quickly connect with job-seekers in many different places, who might not otherwise be contacted by more conventional methods. Small to medium sized enterprises too, find they can compete effectively with larger companies and attract high-calibre recruits to their websites and to the opportunities within their organisations. With regards to cost saving, it has been estimated that expenditure on newspaper advertising and 'head-hunter' fees dropped in the USA by 20 per cent as Internet expenditure increased (Boehle 2000). On-line recruiting, if it is used effectively, is also estimated to cut a week off the recruitment process (Capelli 2001). Large organisations, like L'Oréal and KPMG, justify

use of the Internet to recruit staff on both cost-saving grounds, and because they feel it increases their visibility and attracts high-calibre recruits. With KPMG, for example, the Human Resources staff were dealing with 35,000 paper applications a year, but decided to switch all their UK recruitment online from May 2001 to save time and printing costs (Carter 2001).

7 However, despite the obvious impact the Internet has made on the recruitment process, there are a number of concerns and drawbacks to using this medium. These include the issue of relevance of the medium, confidentiality, the large numbers of applications generated, and the problems that job seekers find in navigating websites and communicating electronically with employers.

8 The first question recruiters need to ask themselves is 'to what extent do members of the target recruitment group have access to the Internet?' Despite increasing use of the Internet, there are still considerable numbers of people, particularly older adults, who do not have access to a personal computer either at work or in their homes. It is estimated, for example, that more than half the adults in just one British region, West Yorkshire, currently do not use the Internet, and that 27 per cent of businesses in the region do not use computers (LSC 2001). It is clear that the Internet is an important way of targeting and contacting applicants for administrative, IT related or senior and middle management posts from across a wide geographical area. However, it is less relevant for contacting applicants for clerical posts and for manual and practical jobs, or for jobs in a specific locality. And even among the target groups, networking and personal contacts, or using trusted professional recruiters, tend to be the strategies most frequently cited as being the most effective for both job-seekers and employers (Feldman and Klass 2002).

9 The issue of confidentiality poses a number of concerns both to job-seekers and employers. In Britain, the Data Protection Act, 1998, stipulates that if a person's details are submitted for one purpose or job, they should not be stored or used for any other purpose without the candidate's permission. However, recruitment agencies or employers may want to retain a candidate's information in case other opportunities arise. Whilst many candidates would not object to this, there have been fears expressed by job-seekers about the commercial use employers or agencies might make of information supplied, or that the information sent electronically could be intercepted by third-parties (Carter 2001).

10 Other pitfalls of using the Internet include processing the large numbers of applications received electronically by large organisations, and the difficulties job-seekers have experienced in using some websites. These difficulties include locating jobs on employer's websites, navigating sites, lack of specific and relevant job descriptions, and difficulties in

customising, formatting and downloading CVs to companies' specifications (Feldman and Klass 2002). Indeed, the problem of processing large numbers of electronic applications has encouraged employers to look at using the Internet more effectively for the selection stages of the recruitment process.

11 Automated filtering of applications is becoming more common through the use of software designed to search CVs for key words or skills. There is in this though, a potential discrimination problem, as all candidates must be given an equal chance to apply, and electronic screening of applications must try and take into account the cultural and language differences of applicants. However, online screening also has the potential to reduce discrimination, as the selection emphasis can be placed less on academic qualifications and more on softer skills, such as team working, negotiating skills and leadership ability. Applicants may also be screened by online verbal, numerical or other psychometric tests, although there is an opportunity here for fraud by some candidates, who might ask a third party to take the tests on their behalf.

12 There are also interesting developments in the use of the Internet for the final selection stages of the recruitment process. Colleagues, separated by distance, can communicate electronically to establish job descriptions and selection criteria, or to view job candidates through video-conferencing. For example, a panel can interview candidates and the interview be relayed to colleagues elsewhere. These distant observers can send their questions or comments to candidates or later pass on their own observations of the interview. Comments sent electronically can also help to reduce discrimination or bias, as these can be recorded and stored: a process which may encourage a more sober and objective assessment of candidates (Tullar and Kaiser 1999).

13 It can be argued that, despite the increase in use of the Internet for recruitment and selection purposes, many Human Resources personnel are still cautious about its use or implementation (Carter 2001). The cost of making the proper investment into the electronic infrastructure is a key prohibiting factor, but another is in the feeling that the Internet should not replace the 'personal touch', particularly in the intermediate or final selection stages. Whilst the Internet can certainly assist in identifying potential candidates, it cannot tell a company how good they are, although, it can certainly facilitate the process of bringing a wide range of opinions of applicants to the final judgement. Whilst the recruitment side of the process is likely to expand and develop in the future, selection of candidates is likely to remain a much more personal affair and in the hands of people, rather than machines.

References

BOEHLE, S. (2000). Online recruiting gets sneaky. *Training*, 37: 66–74.

CAPELLI, P. (2001). Making the most of on-Line recruiting. *Harvard Business Review*, 79 (3): 139–146.

CARTER, M. (2001). We want to be your friend. *Human Resources*, July edition: 33–35.

CHARLES, J. (2000). Finding a job on the web. *Black Enterprises*, 30: 90–95.

DALE, M. (2003). *A Manager's Guide to Recruitment and Selection*, 2nd edn. London: Kogan Page.

FELDMAN, D.C. and KLASS, B.S. (2002). Internet job hunting: a field study of applicant experiences with on-line recruiting. *Human Resources Management*, 41 (2): 175–192.

HR FOCUS (2001). On-line recruiting: what works, what doesn't. March, pp.11–13 (LSC) Learning and Skills Council: *West Yorkshire in focus, 2001: an economic and labour market profile of the sub-region*. Bradford: Learning and Skills Council for West Yorkshire.

INTERNATIONAL DATA CORPORATION (2001). Third annual Email usage forecast and analysis, 2001–2005. Available at http://www.idc.com/home.jhtml [Accessed 12 Dec 2004].

MONDAY, R.W. et al (2002). *Human Resource Management* (8th edn). USA: N.Y: Prentice Hall.

TULLAR, W.L. and KAISER, P.R. (1999). Using new technology: the group support system. In R. Eder, and M. Harris (Eds.) *The Employment Interview Handbook*. London: Sage. (pp. 279–292).

Exercise

An outline of how this essay was structured now follows. Two of the following boxes (for paragraph **six**, and for paragraphs **eight to ten**), are left blank. Read those paragraphs again and summarize in the blank spaces what the writer was trying to do and say in them:

Paragraph 1: Introduction. There is a clear introduction that informs the reader what the essay will attempt to do, e.g. 'describe and evaluate the impact the Internet has had…' etc.

Paragraph 2: Sets the context, e.g. describes the Internet and its rapid advance in recent years.

Paragraphs 3 to 5: Description. How the Internet is currently used for recruitment purposes, e.g. by both employers and job-seekers

Paragraph 6: [Exercise: what was the writer trying to do in this paragraph?]

Paragraph 7: Signals a change of direction and lists the issues to be discussed. (Note the use of the starting word 'However' to alert the reader to this shift in perspective.)

Paragraphs 8–10: [Exercise: what was happening in these paragraphs?]

Paragraphs 11 and 12: Selection issues. Use of the Internet in the selection stage of recruitment and looks at some examples of this.

Paragraph 13: Conclusion. Attempts to pull ideas together and reach a conclusion.

Now look at Appendix 4 for comments on the last exercise.

5.4 Report structure

You may remember from Chapter 2 that the main difference between an essay and a report was that the former gave an opportunity to discuss hypothetical issues, whilst a report is concerned with factual past events.

A good report is like telling a good story. In a report you are telling the reader what happened, why it happened, and presenting facts in an interesting way. Like any good story, you would also set the scene first, making the reader aware of, for example, the historical or other background context.

The contents of any written report should, therefore, be organized into a well structured form. Unless it is a short report, e.g. one page, it is usually necessary to divide information into broad stages, each with its own appropriate subheadings. You will see from the following example report that subheadings are chosen to 'signal' what is to come in any particular stage.

Exercise

An example report follows. It falls into five stages, each containing one or more subheaded sections. There are obvious **introduction** and **conclusion** stages, plus three others. The grid that follows shows the subheadings to look out for within each of these stages. Read the content contained within these subheaded sections and decide what the overall purpose is for each of the other three stages? What does the stage in question **do?**

Write your comments in the right hand column of the grid.

Stage 1: Introduction	
Stage 2 contains the following subheaded sections: • Engineering (worldwide). • The New Strategy. • Engineering UK.	What is the purpose of stage 2 of the report?
Stage 3 contains the following subheaded sections: • Mentoring Scheme. • The Mentoring Scheme in Action.	What is the purpose of stage 3 of the report?
Stage 4 contains the following subheaded section: • Why the Mentoring Scheme Failed.	What is the purpose of stage 4 of the report?
Stage 5: Conclusion	

Now read the report that follows:

Example: report

Case studies often feature in undergraduate and postgraduate courses. Students are usually asked to read a case study and to answer set questions on it, or identify and summarise cause and affect issues. In the example that follows, the student was asked to write a report on the failure of a mentoring scheme in an engineering company. The original case study was quite lengthy and the students set this task were asked to identify and summarise the main reasons for the failure. The challenge for the students was to write a report, as if the tutor was unfamiliar with the case, and to identify and explain the main issues clearly, but within a 1500 word limit.

Title:

Case study report: failure of a mentoring scheme at 'Engineering UK'

Introduction

This report will summarise the key elements that led to the 'withering death' of a mentoring scheme introduced by 'Engineering UK' and is taken from a case study presented by Garvey (1999). Although 'Engineering UK' is an actual company and supplied all the background information, at their request, all company names have been changed.

Engineering (world-wide)

Engineering UK is a satellite company and part of a multi-national engineering network, Engineering (worldwide), which operates in a highly competitive international market. This issue of competition became a major consideration when one competitor made a head-on assault on their customer base. Engineering (worldwide) responded by making an appeal to the workforce to meet the challenge of competition. This was largely achieved within a 30 month period and, as a result, Engineering (worldwide) held its customer base. In order to continue this success, Engineering (worldwide) created a new corporate 'customer led' strategy that senior management hoped would enable them to maintain and quickly develop further the company's world market position.

The new strategy

The communication of this strategy to the satellite companies involved a great number of slogans: 'continuous improvement'; 'benchmarking'; 'learning organisation'; 'common approach'; and 'we're in it for the long haul'. There were also numerous manuals, texts and presentations issued by the parent

---

company, which emphasised the importance of gaining the commitment of the whole workforce and changing company culture to one more responsive and customer oriented. A major training and development programme was established by the parent company to support the strategy.

The programme was aimed at the whole workforce, but there was a clear primary focus on first line supervisors and their team members. At the heart of the development programme the company established a mentoring scheme to support the development of participating individuals. Through this approach of working to a common agenda, Engineering (worldwide) anticipated that all the satellite companies would develop in the same direction and emerge with a shared philosophy.

Engineering UK

Engineering UK had experienced a history of industrial unrest at the time of this initiative. Although by increased efforts it had successfully headed-off the competition it had also, by increasing use of high technology, just reduced the size of the workforce through redundancies. This created the classic fears in the workforce of, 'if we work hard and commission these new machines, we lose our jobs and if we lose our jobs, we become de-skilled'.

There was also some resentment in the company at a lack of sensitivity from management in making people redundant immediately following all the efforts to make the company more efficient. The management of Engineering UK was also characterized by a strong 'command and control' culture that was labelled by some observers as a 'macho-management' style.

Mentoring scheme

The Engineering UK training manager was given the responsibility for introducing a mentoring scheme to the company, which was expected to address the deskilling issue by seeking areas for individual skill development. With fewer people and more technology, the company needed all individuals to be more effective and adaptable at work. The mentoring scheme was expected to help facilitate flexible working and enhance individual performance.

Mentoring involves one person (the mentor) supporting another (the mentee) with career or personal development issues. It should provide a safe environment for both parties to meet, talk in confidence, and for the mentee to set the agenda for discussion on topics relating to his or her personal or career development. It is, or should be, an opportunity for two people to meet as equals, regardless of company rank, and for both to gain from the encounter in their own respective ways.

As noted earlier, there was a strong command and control management structure in the company. However, the training manager envisaged that mentoring would help to change this culture and empower the workforce by giving real authority to both the mentor and mentee (referred to in this company as 'the client'). It would help to create and maintain the 'continuous improvement' process by creating a new learning culture', where opportunities for development would be encouraged. Senior management in the company, recognising the threat from competition and the general directive from Engineering (worldwide) on a need for change, gave their general support to the training manager.

The mentoring scheme in action

The training manager use the Kram (1985) four stage model for introducing the scheme to the company, including defining and communicating to key people involved what mentoring was expected to achieve. The training manager identified the following human resource principles for selecting mentors:

- supportive (of the changes in the organisation);
- status (position in company) – usually workers who were at senior level to the 'client', but not a mentee's direct manager;
- influence (usually meaning experienced in the company and knew the networks and politics of the company);
- secure (established in their career);
- time (willing to put in the time to the scheme);
- Leadership skills.

The training manager began to seek potential mentors for the mentees ('clients') and sent out a list of character attributes and skill criteria to plant managers, asking them to nominate supervisory level staff to be mentors to subordinate colleagues, including staff at other factories up to 300 miles away. Once this was done, mentors were paired with mentees on the basis of a controlled choice: the mentee could choose his/her mentor, but this had to be agreed with both management and mentor. The mentor nominees attended a day and a half training programme to learn the principles of the scheme and to understand their role.

The main focus of the training programme was in explaining the principles of mentoring and the reasons for its introduction. Mentors were asked to support their mentees with issues relating to skill and career development. They were not briefed to control events, but to act as independent counsellors and guides for their mentees. However, mentoring skills were not addressed specifically, as it was assumed that nominee mentors already had the skills necessary by virtue of their experience.

Why the mentoring scheme failed

The mentoring scheme experienced, what was described by the training manager as, a 'withering death'. There were three main reasons why the mentoring scheme at Engineering UK failed.

Firstly, the parent company, Engineering (worldwide) needed to make internal change happen quickly. However, there was a conflict here, as mentor development cannot be hurried (see Kram 1985). There was also a significant residue of cynicism and resentment among the workforce at Engineering UK to overcome that followed in the wake of the redundancies. Mentoring relationships take time to establish; they also need trust between participants, which was lacking in the firm. The Training Officer, whilst identifying suitable personal traits for potential mentors, had to rely on colleagues to match these with existing staff.

Secondly, the 'macho' and hierarchical culture within Engineering UK undermined the values implicit in mentoring, which are based on equal partnerships between people. This led many of the mentors to adopt their normal posture of 'command and control' with their subordinate mentees. This led to many giving advice to mentees, rather than entering into a dialogue with them. The situation was further aggravated by the physical distance between mentors and mentees, which, as noted earlier, included partnerships between some colleagues hundreds of miles apart.

Thirdly, the lack of mentoring skills shown by mentors was clearly a major factor in the downfall of the scheme, but this resulted from the rush to implement the scheme and subsequent inadequate period of training assigned for this purpose. As mentioned earlier, mentoring skills were not addressed, and the day and a half spent on developing the essential understanding of mentoring was clearly inadequate; there was too much for the mentors to understand and change in too short a period. Significant attitudinal change was needed throughout the company – and this was hardly likely to occur in just one and a half days of training.

Conclusion

The expectation of the mentoring scheme within the company as a whole was too great, and did not take into account the variations in company cultures among the satellite companies. In particular, at Engineering UK, there were too many raw wounds from the recent redundancies that needed to be attended to before mentoring had any chance to succeed. Furthermore, the hierarchical structures within this company acted as a barrier to the changes envisaged from mentoring. The 'words of change' were in place, but these had not yet begun to impact on the values and attitudes of existing staff.

References

GARVEY, B. (1999). Let the actions match the words: Engineering UK. In D. MEGGINSON and D. CLUTTERBUCK (Eds.) *Mentoring in action: a practical guide for managers*. London: Kogan Page.

KRAM, K E. (1985). *Mentoring at Work: Developmental Relationships in Organizational Life*. US: Glenview: IL: Foresman.

5.4.1 Comment

As shown, there are five stages in the report. There is an **introduction**, **background** information, **main issues** presented (the mentoring scheme presented), and a **discussion** on why the scheme failed. Finally, there is a **conclusion** that summarizes the main reasons for the early demise of the mentoring scheme. The limited number of references – just two sources – is explained by the fact that this was a report on a case study, which required the study to concentrate on just the issues raised in the case study supplied.

The report is written in a clear, direct way and in the third person. The student does not overdo the use of bullet points and has concentrated on presenting the main issues in a well organized way.

5.4.2 Stages of reports

Most reports will contain a five or six stage structure. Reports can be categorized into two main groups: those involving investigation or enquiry of some sort, and those that present a summary or synopsis of an event. In a relatively short (non-dissertation) report the main stages are shown, as follows:

Investigatory report	Other reports
1 Introduction 2 Background information 3 Methods and materials 4 Results 5 Discussion 6 Conclusion	1 Introduction 2 Background Information 3 Main issues 4 Discussion 5 Conclusion

You would also include a list of evidence and other source **references**, written in the referencing style adopted by your institution or department.

5.4.3 More detail on these stages

Introduction

In the introduction section of your report you would normally introduce the aim and subject of the report to tell the reader what to expect: what issues are being explored or evaluated and, if necessary, why. It can also be helpful to summarize the main stages of the report and the focus of each.

Background information

In this section of the report you would present an overview of the main factors leading to the report. These can include historic, scientific/technical, economic, political, or social influences, and other macro or micro factors that enable the reader to put the main report issues into a context or perspective. In some reports you may also want to summarize the findings of previous research or investigation in the topic area. In a long report, or dissertation, this often has its own section, i.e. entitled 'Literature review'.

Main issues, methods, and materials

1 **Main issues**. In this broad area of a non-investigatory report, you would outline the **main issues** that are the central focus and concern.
2 **Methods/materials**. In an investigatory or technical/scientific report you would present details about the research or experiment to allow others to replicate the work in the future. You would summarize in chronological order what you did, giving essential information, as in this extract from a student dissertation report: 'A CPD plan and record file composed by the RPSGB was obtained from a tutor, which was analysed. To gain some understanding with regards to views on CPD, a handful of local community pharmacists were then approached. However, this open and randomised method proved not to be very effective, as views were very limited in parts and broadened in others'.
The items and elements you could include in this methods or materials section are, as follows:

* The research approach adopted and the reasons for this. If in retrospect you feel it was not the correct approach, you should say so, and state why.
* If applicable, the materials used in any physical testing process.
* The **methods** you used to gather primary and/or secondary data, and why you chose those particular methods.
* The criteria you adopted for collecting this data (e.g. target number, age, gender, occupation, etc) giving reasons for your choice.
* The target sample number and type of sample, e.g. a random sample.
* The actual number you achieved and the reasons for any shortfall.
* Where you collected the data.
* When you collected it, if relevant.
* Who was involved in the collection, if relevant.
* How it was collected.
* The logistical or other problems encountered in collecting or analysing it, if applicable.
* How you collated and categorized the data.

Results

The results section presents a summary of the data or other information you gathered. At this stage of the report you present and summarize the data or information without going into detailed discussion of the implications of your findings; this information goes into the next 'Discussion' section.

So, in the 'Results' section you could include the following information:

* Summary of the statistical data gathered.
* If applicable, how and why the results were affected by any event, situation, or phenomenon within or outside your control.
* If there was a shortfall in the amount of data you gained, how you compensated or dealt with this.
* How the amount of data collected by you compares or contrasts with previous research in this area of enquiry.

Discussion

This section explains, analyses, and discusses the result, including implications of your findings. It can present, if applicable, some resolution or answers to the main research questions. You may also want or need to connect the result in some way to the theories, models, and practices that you introduced in the earlier background sections.

You could include the following into a 'Discussion' section of a report:

* How the findings connect with your overall research aim and research questions.
* How and why your findings connect with previous research.
* What the findings mean in theory and/or practice.
* How unexpected/expected were some or all of the findings?
* How the findings might be applied.
* When they might be applied (the context).
* Who might apply them.
* Any recommendations you might make based on your research findings.
* What future research might be conducted to build on what you have done.

Conclusions, summary, or recommendations

The introduction of your report was the place to tell the reader what you are going to say. The conclusion is an opportunity to **remind** readers what you have told them. This may sound trite, but it is important to do this, as it reinforces the important points you made earlier in the report. An effective conclusion leaves the reader with a sense of completion.

5.4.4 Some additional sections you might include – depending on the length and nature of the report

Abstract or summary

In longer reports it is common to have an abstract or summary page. This is a brief summary of the aim of the report, methodology, if applicable, and the results or conclusions reached. An abstract or summary would normally be no more than a page in length. Check with your tutor to see if you need to include this with your report. It would not normally be included in short reports, but would undoubtedly be expected in dissertation project reports.

Contents page

In a lengthy report you would normally include a contents page, which would include main chapter headings, any subdivisions within these and page numbers. These chapter headings can be numbered and given numerical sub-divisions, for example:

1 Introduction
2 Organization background

   2.1 History
   2.2 Geographical features
   2.3 Current networks
   2.4 Structure of organization

3 Current challenges facing organization

   3.1 Competition
   3.2 Changes in market
   3.3 Technological changes, [etc . . .]

You may also be expected to link the headings and subheadings to page numbers to assist a reader to quickly find a particular section of the report.

Appendices

The Appendix is the place for lengthy and detailed material that would inter-fere with the easy flow of reading in the main body of the report. It may contain important data that you refer to in your report – but the main text should be used to summarize this key information.

   The appendix items are there for readers to look at if they wish, particularly if they wanted to check the accuracy and validity of your report discussion or conclusions.

The appendix would, for example, contain detailed statistical data, computer programs, and examples of questionnaires used in any research project.

Main points in this chapter:

- Good essay structure starts with a close examination of the title and all the issues raised by it.
- A paragraph in an essay will contain a single idea. The idea is usually introduced in the first or second sentence, then expanded.
- Your ideas should cascade from one paragraph to the next: a concluding sentence or idea in one paragraph will be picked up by the next, and so on to the conclusion.
- Reports can be presented in a broad five or six stage structure.
- Subheadings can be used to separate out stages of a report into subsections.
- The introduction paragraph or section in an assignment is a particularly important one – because this is the first impression of you as a writer.

6

'You did not tell me anything new'

Become an ideas entrepreneur • The role of a student • What is creativity?
• Looking good

This chapter is about:

- Finding new approaches, interpretations, and insights to subjects studied.
- Becoming more creative with ideas.
- Being creative in the way assignments are presented.

'You did not tell me anything new'. This type of feedback comment can confound students, particularly those who have gained good marks in past assignments for describing or reproducing faithfully and accurately what they have read or learned from their tutors. So what does it mean? Comments like this may be given if you play safe and simply summarize what the tutor has said in lectures or tutorials, or paraphrase what you read in set texts, but without taking your engagement with the subject beyond this.

One student I had contacted wanted clarification from the tutor about what was meant by this comment. The tutor wrote back:

> You are also very likely to get a good mark if you tell me something new; by, for example, either going off the reading list to bring in new relevant work, or through use of examples to illustrate and support arguments.

Work that offers new integrative models or attempts to synthesize different ideas is also likely to hit the button in this regard.

Other related comments from tutors might be that your work 'lacked originality', or was not 'creative' in its interpretation or problem solving approaches. So what can you do to address this type of criticism?

There are three possible approaches to take, as suggested by the tutor's comments:

1 Look for new insights, interpretations, and approaches to the topic by reading beyond the recommended reading list.
2 Look for examples, particularly unusual ones, to illustrate the way theories, ideas, models, or practices can be applied in the real world.
3 Think of creative and original ways to interpret and apply ideas. This can be an important opportunity for you to rise above the ideas advanced by others, and to become an 'ideas entrepreneur'.

6.1 Become an ideas entrepreneur

An ideas entrepreneur is someone who is not afraid to **take risks with ideas**. You may remember from Chapter 2 that the students most likely to gain A grades were the 'explorers', brave enough to venture into the academic 'territory' others did not. They were likely to have been creative with established ideas or practices, yet done so in a thorough, analytical, and objective way. They were likely too, to have made connections between different ideas and concepts and presented an original perspective on the subject.

This risk taking, as in life outside the university, may not always pay off; some tutors may remain unimpressed with your ideas or may not be convinced by your analysis. But many of your tutors, despite outward appearances, have often been, and many still are, risk takers themselves with ideas, and do respect students who have a different, but intelligent perspective on things, **and can back up their ideas with sound, reliable evidence**. Being wacky is not enough; but being wacky and well read is another matter. So becoming an ideas entrepreneur involves you thinking about your 'role' as a student.

6.2 The role of a student

What is your role as a student?

This may seem like a strange question, and a first reaction might be to say 'to learn'. But this raises a second question – about learning. There are many different ways to learn and these can be connected with the idea of a student successfully playing different metaphorical professional roles – and particularly in relation to writing assignments. The mnemonic **JADE** summarizes these roles:

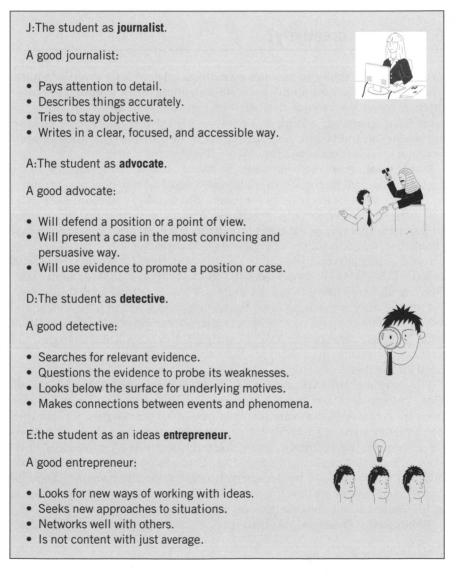

J:The student as **journalist**.

A good journalist:

- Pays attention to detail.
- Describes things accurately.
- Tries to stay objective.
- Writes in a clear, focused, and accessible way.

A:The student as **advocate**.

A good advocate:

- Will defend a position or a point of view.
- Will present a case in the most convincing and persuasive way.
- Will use evidence to promote a position or case.

D:The student as **detective**.

A good detective:

- Searches for relevant evidence.
- Questions the evidence to probe its weaknesses.
- Looks below the surface for underlying motives.
- Makes connections between events and phenomena.

E:the student as an ideas **entrepreneur**.

A good entrepreneur:

- Looks for new ways of working with ideas.
- Seeks new approaches to situations.
- Networks well with others.
- Is not content with just average.

Students may be conscientious with the **'JAD'** dimensions, but often neglect the **'E'**: **ideas entrepreneur** approach to learning.

But can you learn to be creative? Everyone has the ability to be creative – remember how creative children can be, if encouraged. Creativity has often been suppressed within adults by the conventions and routines of everyday life; but it is still there and can be re-awakened.

6.3 What is creativity?

Creativity is the ability to produce something original for a given situation. Creativity is not just the ability to create something out of nothing, but more often involves the mental flexibility to generate and apply new ideas by combining, changing, adding to, or reapplying existing ones. Some creative approaches are brilliant in their originality, while others are just good, simple, practical ideas that make you say, 'Why didn't I think of that?'

Don't think, therefore, you have to be of 'artistic' temperament to be creative. You can, of course, think laterally and look for new opportunities to connect ideas, or to create new models. But equally, and more likely, you can arrive at creative ideas by systematic, logical, and structured approaches to problems that can reveal flaws in existing ideas, which can generate new problem solving approaches or perspectives to them.

In the academic world you can be creative with theories, models, ideas, and practice (TMIPs). Don't forget what the tutor at the start of this chapter said: 'You are also very likely to get a good mark if you tell me something new'. Telling the tutor 'something new', however, requires you to have a clear and knowledgeable grasp on what is already there. Once you have a clear grasp of what happens, then you can look at existing TMIPs from different angles, add to them, connect them to other practices and ideas, and generally try to take a fresh look at them.

This is where the 'JAD' aspects of the student roles connect with the 'E' ideas entrepreneur and creative process. Creative thinking is not separate from critical analysis, but is another tributary of it. Futurologists, for example, don't merely guess at what the future will bring, they base their predictions on past and present economic, social, and cultural trends. Creative ideas, however, as suggested earlier, can expand these trends by looking at them from different perspectives, or by deconstructing old ideas and reshaping them in line with contemporary developments. The iPod, for example, is an extension of the Walkman, but one that drew on advances in electronics.

To be creative, therefore, you need to:

- Really know your subject.
- Learn techniques to develop creative ways of thinking.
- Practice these techniques.
- Be prepared to step outside a 'safe' mode of responses to problem solving.

In relation to assignment writing, here are two techniques to try:

- The 'What's missing' (WM) approach.
- The four-way thinking approach.

6.3.1 What's missing? (WM) approach

You will undoubtedly be presented with a range of theories, models, ideas, and practices (TMIPs) on your course and asked to apply them to real life situations. With the WM approach, always ask yourself, 'Is anything missing from this TMIP?'

You can try this approach with two familiar models used for analysis purposes in a range of subject disciplines and situations:

- PEST analysis
- SWOT analysis

PEST analysis

The **PEST** analysis is a well known tool for understanding the political, economic, socio-cultural, and technological background for any business or other project related situation you are considering in a particular country.

The four **PEST** dimensions would include the following elements:

Political, e.g.:	**Economic**, e.g.:
• Type of government, including stability.	• Main industries.
• Type of legal system.	• Skills of workforce.
• Freedoms of citizens.	• Current inflation.
• Likely changes in near future.	• Transport infrastructures.
Socio-cultural, e.g.:	**Technological**, e.g.:
• Demographic trends.	• Emerging technologies.
• Mobility of population.	• Impact of new technology.
• Employment patterns.	• Research and development activity.
• Lifestyle trends.	• Future technological trends.

Exercise

This is obviously a useful model as a framework for identifying the characteristics of a country or region and drawing conclusions as to the significant forces affecting its current and future development. However, might there be other dimensions you could consider to make the analysis model more comprehensive in its coverage? Write any other dimension(s) that occur to you in the space that follows:

```
┌─────────────────────────────────────────────────────────────┐
│                                                             │
│                                                             │
│                                                             │
│                                                             │
│                                                             │
│                                                             │
│                                                             │
│                                                             │
└─────────────────────────────────────────────────────────────┘
```

SWOT analysis

The SWOT analysis is widely used to identify the strengths, weaknesses, opportunities, and threats of any situation, including individual circumstances. A SWOT analysis, for example, of a business or commercial project might include:

Strengths	Weaknesses
• Unique selling points.	• Negative customer feedback.
• Positive customer feedback.	• Price range of products, e.g. too high.
• Product range.	• Poor location, etc.

Opportunities	Threats
• Potential for expansion.	• Strong competition from other retailers.
• Future markets.	• Economic downturn.
• Favourable social and economic trends.	• Lack of qualified staff.

Exercise

Again, the SWOT Analysis is a useful framework for strategic analysis of any given situation. But are there other elements that could be added to make it more comprehensive in its coverage? If so, what are they and why should they be added?

```
┌─────────────────────────────────────────────────────────────┐
│                                                             │
│                                                             │
│                                                             │
│                                                             │
│                                                             │
│                                                             │
│                                                             │
│                                                             │
│                                                             │
│                                                             │
└─────────────────────────────────────────────────────────────┘
```

Now look at Appendix 5 for comments on this **PEST** and **SWOT** exercise.

6.3.2 Four-way thinking approach

Another approach is to adopt a 'four-way thinking' approach to problem solving (Rose 2000). It does not work for all assignment questions or tasks, particularly those where you are asked to describe existing phenomena, but it can work when you are asked to discuss and suggest solutions to a problem, resolve a particular dilemma, or present a new strategy.

The four ways are:

1 Front-to-back thinking.
2 Top–down thinking.
3 Back-to-front thinking.
4 Bottom–up thinking.

Front-to-back thinking

This approach **starts with the situation** or problem and works systematically toward a solution or explanation. This involves a DANCE approach.

D **Defining** the problem or situation.
A **Alternatives**: generating lots of alternative situations/solutions.
N **Narrowing** down the alternatives.
C **Choosing** one and checking out the consequences.
E **Effect**: putting ideas into effect.

Top–down thinking

This way of thinking takes an overview position and imagines you are looking at a situation in a detached way and ready to see other people's viewpoints, and particularly those who may be directly affected and involved as participants. This is a particularly good position to take if you are personally committed to a particular argument or practice in an assignment, as it forces you to be more objective.

Good questions to ask:

• How would a detached observer see this situation?
• Are there other underlying issues to consider?
• How would it feel to be affected by any changes proposed?
• What do the direct opponents of any position think or feel about any proposed change?
• Is there a compromise situation?

Back-to-front thinking

With this approach you **start** with the desired solution and work backwards to envisage how it might come about in the future.

Questions to ask include:

- What does 'success' look and feel like?
- What is standing in the way of the solution I want or feel is best?
- What is the simplest way of removing these obstacles?
- What are the stages I have to go through (backwards) to bring the idea to fruition?
- Who or what could help in making the path easy for this solution?

Bottom–up thinking

This 'bottom–up' way of thinking turns a problem, issue, or situation upside down and asks or poses different questions, or looks at a situation in a completely different way to the norm. Try this exercise.

Exercise

You are probably reading this book because you are dissatisfied with your grades and you are seeking advice and techniques to improve them. You may think, 'Well, this guy must be an expert, so I will try his ideas'. But imagine **you** are the expert and you have been asked to deliver a brief talk to other students on how they could improve their grades. What would advice to them be, based on your own experiences?

6.4 Looking good

You can also enhance creativity if your assignment is also **presented** in a way that commands interest and attention from any reader. It will not save you from a poor mark if the work is unsound, but if your arguments are valid, an attractive presentation can add an additional positive element to it. One important dimension to good presentation is your choice of word processing typefaces and type sizes.

Sometimes specific advice is given by an institution, or by your module tutor, on which typefaces are permissible – and clearly in this situation you will have limited choices. Many students too, simply use the default typeface and typesize setting on their personal computer to prepare their assignments. However, there is some evidence suggesting that typography has a psychological impact on readers, so it may be worth experimenting with different typefaces, providing this is acceptable within university course regulations, or to your module tutor.

Exercise

Look at the following at the following extracts that are printed in different typefaces. Which do you like best for overall legibility and appearance?

1. Creativity does not mean being impractical. A firm knowledge of basic ideas and practices is essential to creativity as it informs you of what is possible now or from the past. Creative ideas, however, as suggested earlier, can expand these possibilities by reshaping them or looking at them from different perspectives.	2. Creativity does not mean being impractical. A firm knowledge of basic ideas and practices is essential to creativity as it informs you of what is possible now or from the past. Creative ideas, however, as suggested earlier, can expand these possibilities by reshaping them or looking at them from different perspectives.
3. Creativity does not mean being impractical. A firm knowledge of basic ideas and practices is essential to creativity as it informs you of what is possible now or from the past. Creative ideas, however, as suggested earlier, can expand these possibilities by reshaping them or looking at them from different perspectives.	4. Creativity does not mean being impractical. A firm knowledge of basic ideas and practices is essential to creativity as it informs you of what is possible now or from the past. Creative ideas, however, as suggested earlier, can expand these possibilities by reshaping them or looking at them from different perspectives.

5. Creativity does not mean being impractical. A firm knowledge of basic ideas and practices is essential to creativity as it informs you of what is possible now or from the past. Creative ideas, however, as suggested earlier, can expand these possibilities by reshaping them or looking at them from different perspectives.	6. Creativity does not mean being impractical. A firm knowledge of basic ideas and practices is essential to creativity as it informs you of what is possible now or from the past. Creative ideas, however, as suggested earlier, can expand these possibilities by reshaping them or looking at them from different perspectives.
7. Creativity does not mean being impractical. A firm knowledge of basic ideas and practices is essential to creativity as it informs you of what is possible now or from the past. Creative ideas, however, as suggested earlier, can expand these possibilities by reshaping them or looking at them from different perspectives.	8. Creativity does not mean being impractical. A firm knowledge of basic ideas and practices is essential to creativity as it informs you of what is possible now or from the past. Creative ideas, however, as suggested earlier, can expand these possibilities by reshaping them or looking at them from different perspectives.

The eight extracts above are examples of typefaces found on most personal computers. Which do you like the best for legibility and attractiveness on the page? In the space below, rank the eight extracts, in order of preference.

Say why you ranked the first two at the top of your list:

6.4.1 Commentary

The typefaces

In the order presented, the typefaces in the exercise were:

1   Times New Roman (size 12)

2   Courier New (size 11)

3   Arial (size 11)

4   Tahoma (size 11)

5   **Comic Sans Ms (size 11)**

6   *Monotype Corsiva (size 12)*

7   Georgia (size 11)

8   Verdana (size 11)

A comparison study in 2001 (Bernard et al. 2001) found that examples number 8 (Verdana), 3 (Arial), and 5 (Comic Sans Ms) were the ones most frequently selected for legibility and impact in a business or personal context. However, numbers 1 (Times New Roman) and 2 (Courier New) were perceived as more 'business like'.

Aric Sigman, an American psychologist, who has made a study of the social and emotional connotations of typefaces, recommends the use of Times New Roman, in typeface size 11 or 12, for more conservative writing, or as a generally 'safe option'. Both studies agree that the more ornate or flowery typefaces (as in example 6) are not suitable for assignments, or for use in CVs.

However, Sigman feels that Verdana, Arial, Comic Sans, or Tahoma can be used where a 'contemporary feel' is desired (Sigman 2001). This advice may be worth bearing in mind for assignments where you are making an effort to say something different, and where you want the presentational aspects of your writing to contribute to this originality.

Main points in this chapter:

- The way to avoid criticism that you are not telling the tutor something new is to read beyond your recommended reading lists (see next chapter), and to think about the way ideas can be applied, connected to other ideas, or reinterpreted.
- Creativity is not just about coming up with new ideas, it is more often about looking at old ideas in new ways.
- Creativity in an academic context can involve taking risks with ideas. Your tutor may not agree with your analysis, but will certainly respect it if you can back up your position with sound evidence and logical argument.
- You may have some flexibility in the way your assignment is presented in terms of typeface settings. If so, think about the emotional impact typefaces have on the reader.

7

'Your reading for this assignment is limited'

Which sources to use • Weaker sources? • Other sources • How can you discriminate and choose between sources?

This chapter is about:

- The difference between primary and secondary sources.
- Which sources to use in evidence, and when to use them.
- How to evaluate the quality of sources, particularly those from the Internet.

It is a less common expression now, but the term 'reading', when applied to university study, can refer to the subject of your degree, as in the statement: 'I am reading history at XYZ University'. This usage of the word developed because the reading of printed sources, mainly text books, was such an integral part of degree level study. It still is, but today the range of sources available to you since the mid-1990s has broadened considerably with the expansion of electronic communication. A vast range of sources can be found on the Internet and information can now be readily heard, seen, and watched – as well as read. And perhaps it is **because** of the range of information available that tutors make comments such as, 'Your reading for this assignment is limited'. The contemporary world of information appears to be like the proverbial Bible land 'flowing with milk and honey' to the point that you can easily lose track of what is important, and what is not.

You can, for example, get sidetracked into using minor or secondary sources, when you should be using those with a more primary evidential role to play. This can result in a tutor writing on a feedback sheet: 'The secondary sources are intended to supplement the primary sources and guide you in your reading. They should be read judiciously and not treated as authoritative. Nobody's opinions (even the lecturer's) are more valid than the sources on which they are based (Tutor quoted in Clanchy and Ballard 1998: 8).

7.1 Which sources to use

The tutor quoted mentions primary and secondary sources. What is the difference?

Primary sources	Secondary sources
This is evidence that comes directly from the people involved in the event or phenomenon in question. This would include theories, models, ideas, interpretations, definitions, and practices as described and presented by their originators, rather than commentators.	This includes material produced about the event or phenomenon, including the commentary or interpretation of others about theories, models, ideas, definitions, and practices. It would include, for example, reportage material in newspapers, magazines, reference books, and on the Internet.

One commentator, Campion (1997), asserts that preference should be given to work that is:

- Seminal in an area of research.
- Methodologically or conceptually rigorous.
- Most recent.

When writing this, Campion had psychology, his own subject, in mind and based his arguments on the comments he canvassed and received from 300 reviewers of the journal *Personnel Psychology*, and the boards of *Journal of Applied Psychology*, *Academy of Management Journal*, and *Academy of Management Review*. So how valid are Campion's comments for other subject areas? Let us look at each of these main sources, plus some others that Campion does not specifically mention, e.g. Internet sites.

7.1.1 'Seminal in an area of research'

This refers to primary sources that have had a significant impact in any subject area and are the foundation for later research or debate by the originator or others. This seminal work might be presented in written or other creative forms, e.g. music, art, or dance. Most tutors in all subject areas are likely to agree that seminal work should be regarded as primary sources of evidence for assignments.

7.1.2 'Methodologically or conceptually rigorous'

This is primary source work that has been subjected to the critical scrutiny of others in the same or related fields of study. Often this activity will take the form of building on or testing seminal work in the subject area. The purpose, background, methodology, analysis, and results of a particular piece of work will usually be presented to an academic community and the findings debated. Typically, this work will be reported in peer reviewed journals, presented at conferences, or published in book form, particularly books produced by academic or other research institutions.

Most tutors in all subject areas are likely to agree that this type of peer reviewed work should be regarded as a primary source of evidence for assignments.

7.1.3 'Most recent'

Here we can find a division between subject areas. Not all tutors would agree that 'most recent' is always an essential component of strong evidence. With disciplines such as philosophy, English, religious study, law, and accounting, the 'most recent' can be less applicable, and more emphasis may be placed on seminal work in these disciplines, particularly on books.

However, some disciplines, such as business, sciences, information technology, psychology, and communication studies, are subject to powerful contemporary influences and the 'most recent' evidence is likely to apply – but not always. Even in these fields it is worth looking at what happened in the past to explore how contemporary ideas have built on, or responded to, these earlier ideas, models, and practices.

To identify current thinking, even in the slower changing subject areas, peer reviewed journals are useful sources for assignments. Your tutor will tell you which these are, and you should be able to access them electronically through your institution's library. The importance of using journals in assignments was highlighted in a study by Zeegers and Giles (1996), which analysed essays submitted by over 500 first year undergraduate biology students. A positive correlation was found for the relationship between the number of relevant journal articles referred to in the assignment and the level of mark awarded: 'Most students who were awarded a credit grade or higher used five journal articles or more and spent on average 20 hours reading them' (p. 452). The number of relevant journal articles read and the number of hours spent reading generally, and writing the essay, appears also to have been a significant factor in the award of good marks to geography students (Hounsel 1984), as well as to psychology students (Norton 1990).

7.2 Weaker sources?

Campion argues that 'the following sources are not considered [to offer] strong support' as evidence in assignments:

- Statements made in research articles that are not findings.
- Textbooks.
- Professional or trade journals, and similar sources.
- Newspapers and other popular press sources.

Although Campion offers a useful starting point for identifying 'weaker' sources, much depends on the context in which these are used as evidence. Indeed, this is a point Campion recognizes himself: 'the quality of a reference depends on the context within which it is being used. If it is appropriate to the context, then it is a good quality reference, e.g. popular press references may be appropriate to show public awareness of an issue' (p. 166).

So with that in mind let us look at each of the sources he specifically mentions.

7.2.1 Statements 'made in research articles that are not findings'

Campion has in mind assertions or conclusions by an author that are unsubstantiated (i.e. with no valid evidence to support them). Most of your tutors would agree that this type of comment needs to be treated with caution rather than as hard evidence in your assignments. The important question for you to ask then is, 'Where or what is the evidence to support this assertion?' This question is relevant no matter how important or significant the author in question appears to be in the subject area.

7.2.2 'Textbooks'

The term 'textbooks' is rather ambiguous and we need to distinguish between textbooks that:

- Summarize the work of a range of authors in a particular subject area; and
- Edited books that present a collection of original articles written by a range of specialists in a particular field.

Summary texts

Summaries of the work of authors can be an excellent starting point for gaining an overview of a subject area. However, these are secondary sources and, wherever possible, you should look at the original work that inspired the summary and use this as primary source material in your assignments.

There are three main reasons for this. First, the summary may not always completely and accurately reflect what the original author said. Second, the original work may contain qualifying clauses, particular examples, or other additional material, which may be omitted in the summary text, but which you might find helpful to include in your assignment. And third, reference to the original text demonstrates your commitment to the subject: it suggests that you are motivated and interested enough in the subject to seek and check out the original work for yourself.

However, there are circumstances when it would be appropriate to use the secondary source in a textbook like this:

- If you find it difficult to find or gain access to the primary source.
- If you are confident that the secondary source authors are reliable and accurate in the way they have summarized, paraphrased, or quoted the original authors: your tutor, for example, may have recommended the textbook.
- If you do not need to go into any great depth of analysis on what the primary author has written.

Edited texts

In the case of an edited book of original articles, however, these can often be treated as primary work, providing the authors have taken the opportunity to present research findings for the first time or to take a fresh approach to the topic. You need, however, to check whether or not the view expressed is being presented for the first time, as sometimes authors will simply rehash ideas presented elsewhere in an earlier work. The author concerned will probably state to what extent the ideas presented are new, and the list of references or bibliography at the end of the chapter will also give you a clue to the extent of their originality, as earlier published work by the author will undoubtedly be listed.

7.2.3 'Professional or trade journals and similar sources'

These tend to be journals or magazines that carry a range of articles written in a journalistic style, and which simply report what is happening in any particular profession.

Most tutors would agree these journals should be treated with caution as primary sources. For example, statistical evidence presented in these journals has usually originated from external and published research rather than from the journal concerned, although there can be exceptions to this rule. If the statistics have originated elsewhere, you really need to seek out and read the original source and present this as your primary evidence. Occasionally, however, an influential commentator in a particular profession may write an original article for the journal, or make a controversial point, that you might want to use as an illustration or in support of a particular argument.

7.2.4 'Newspapers and other popular press sources'

Although most tutors would agree on the secondary role of newspapers as evidence, it is possible to find authoritative and original articles by prominent commentators in the more serious newspapers, particularly in the arts, humanities, science, and business worlds, that could be treated as primary sources. Newspapers are most likely to report on research rather than instigate it themselves, although the more serious broadsheet newspaper may occasionally launch a campaign on a particular topic and gather independent research evidence itself.

7.3 Other sources

You will undoubtedly encounter a wide range of other sources, such as:

- Notes supplied by a lecturer.
- Reference books.
- Autobiographies or biographies.
- Reports.
- Internet and other electronic sources.

So what is the status of these sources as evidence in assignments? Again, this depends on the context in which they are being used, but here are some general guidelines.

7.3.1 Notes supplied by a lecturer

These are usually summaries of lectures or tutorials, and rarely contain original material. Most tutors would expect you to use them as a guide to finding original and reading sources and for revision purposes, but not for use as primary evidence. If, however, a tutor does pass his or her own comment on the subject, you might want to use this as either secondary or primary evidence, depending on the authority and experience of the lecturer in the subject area.

7.3.2 Reference books

Reference books, including dictionaries and encyclopaedias, can be helpful in finding factual information that can be used for secondary background purposes. They can also be helpful in identifying key commentators and primary sources. Many specialist dictionaries are compiled by leading authorities in their fields (e.g. music, art, and sciences), and the introduction sections of these books can be very useful as secondary, or sometimes even primary, sources for the authoritative commentaries they present on developments in the subject area.

7.3.3 Autobiographies or biographies

All autobiographies and biographies should be treated with caution as evidence of 'true' accounts of what actually happened! Autobiographies can be treated as primary sources if they are written by a person that is the focus of your study. But it is often interesting to compare a version of an event described in an autobiography with those of other sources. Different perceptions and recollections can emerge of the same event. It is wise, therefore, to read as widely as possible and then to present your summary with a fair degree of cautious objectivity.

7.3.4 Reports

Many reports can be treated as 'strong' primary evidence sources, particularly those commissioned by government, official agencies, or other interested organizations. However, even official reports should be subject to the same scrutiny by you to ensure that they are 'methodologically or conceptually rigorous' in their investigations and balanced in their comments. The way the report was conducted, who was involved, over what time scale, and who funded or commissioned it, should all be kept in mind and discussed in your assignment. If this information is missing, you need to treat the findings with caution.

7.3.5 Internet and other electronic sources

Primary evidence can be found on the Internet, but it can rub shoulders with material that is unreliable, wrong, or even plain crazy. When you read books, journals, and other resources that have been subject to the critical review of others, at least some quality filters have been applied to remove or highlight material that fails this scrutiny test. But the Internet has presented a wonderful opportunity for assorted egoists to send out opinionated junk into the wide blue yonder.

Nevertheless, useful evidence for assignments can still be found on the Internet, including articles written by authors respected in their fields, electronic journals carrying quality and peer reviewed articles, reports from prestigious agencies, government papers, company data, access to conference papers, and commentary from professional institutions.

Primary sources are clearly a significant factor in this process, but how do you select the best material, particularly if you are faced with a wide choice?

7.4 How can you discriminate and choose between sources?

Faced with a mass of primary source material, how can you discriminate and choose between them? For both electronic and printed sources there are essentially three connected areas of enquiry to help you select the best evidence for your assignments. The first two, expertise of author and credibility of source, will help you determine which sources to choose if more than one appears relevant to the point you are making.

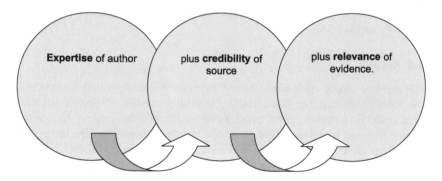

Expertise of author

plus **credibility** of source

plus **relevance** of evidence.

You can ask the following questions of all sources.

7.4.1 Expertise of author

General questions:

- What qualifications and experience does the author/originator have?
- Is the author well known in his or her field?
- Do other writers in the field of study refer to this author in their work?
- Do your tutors mention this author?

And, in addition, for electronic information:

- Is it clear who is taking 'ownership' of the online information presented?
- Is there a link to any named author's email address?

7.4.2 Credibility of source

General questions:

- Is the publisher/originator of the evidence a reputable one?
- Are sources of evidence presented in a credible way, e.g. properly referenced?
- Does the bibliography presented by the author seem comprehensive in its coverage?
- Does the author present all relevant background and contextual information for the ideas presented, e.g. does the author explain in a convincing way the rationale for his or her ideas?
- Is the information presented still valid? For example, if it was written over five years ago are the ideas still applicable today?
- If it is a research finding, is the methodology presented and discussed?

And in addition for electronic information:

- Do your tutors recommend this Internet site?
- Why has this site been established – is it clear from the introduction?
- Who sponsors and/or pays for the site?
- Who is the intended readership for the site?
- Are there any open or possible biases in the site?
- Were you linked to this site from a reliable source?
- Does it **look** professional?
- Is the site easy to navigate and use?
- Can it be used easily by people with visual and/or auditory disabilities?
- Does the resource follow good principles of design with proper grammar, spelling, and style?
- Was the site updated recently?

7.4.3 Relevance of evidence

The first two elements connect with this third key criterion for selecting evidence. Whether it is from a printed or electronic source, the expertise of the author and credibility of source are your first considerations – then finalize your choice by the source that presents the most relevant evidence to the point you are making.

Main points from this chapter

- Try and use **primary** sources whenever possible in your assignments for your central definitions, main descriptions, quotations, key points, arguments, and assertions; and **secondary** material for lesser definitions, factual information, illustrative examples, and supporting points.
- Peer reviewed journal articles are a particularly relevant and useful source of contemporary discussion and debate in your subject area.
- When selecting sources for assignments, three elements should be considered in this order: (1) expertise of author or originator; (2) credibility of source; and (3) the relevance of the evidence to the point being made in the assignment.

8

'You need to improve your referencing'

Using evidence in assignments • Why reference? • When to reference • When you don't need to reference • Avoiding plagiarism • How to reference • What's the difference between references and a bibliography?

This chapter is about:

- Why, when, and how to reference your sources.
- How to avoid plagiarism.
- Demonstrating referencing in action.

8.1 Using evidence in assignments

Using evidence effectively by referencing sources in assignments is an essential skill for higher education. But students may not always be given a complete rationale for referencing by their tutors and may struggle to understand the 'when to' as well as the 'how to' aspects of it. This can lead to mistakes. One study, for example, of referencing errors in doctoral dissertation proposals submitted by 64 students found that one in three sources cited contained a referencing error of some sort, either in the intext citation or in the full list of references (Waytowich et al. 2006).

However, professional academic writers are not immune from making mistakes. Gosling et al. (2004), in a study of reference and quotation accuracy in four peer reviewed manual therapy journals, found nearly 36 percent of errors in 115 sources cited. Another study of a sample of 200 references, taken from papers published in ophthalmic journals, found 35 errors in the way sources were referenced and 30 inaccuracies in quotations used (Buchan et al. 2005).

This has concerned many academics, and Harzing (2002), for example, has argued that good referencing is essential to maintain the trust and credibility of the reader, who is reliant on the author to present knowledge in an objective and reliable way. The importance of accurate referencing to good assignment results has also been suggested in studies done by Norton (1990), Zeegers and Giles (1996), and Angélil-Carter (2000). For example, Zeegers and Giles suggest that 'high distinction and distinction students' are distinguishable from students who achieved a lower grade by, amongst other things, 'having less difficulty writing references' (1996: 451). Angélil-Carter quotes a feedback comment from a tutor to a student:

> This is an excellent exposition and why oh why is it not properly referenced? Please resubmit with proper referencing so that I can give you the 80% you certainly should have. By not referencing you strip it of its academic value and you lose its value for yourself and the audience i.e. myself as reader (2000: 65–6).

Angélil-Carter talks of the 'academic value' of referencing, and she also suggests that students do have a general sense of why referencing is important: 'Students overwhelmingly understand that the role of referencing is one of display of coverage of the readings, of indicating for the tutor that you have read the required readings, or perhaps read more than the required readings' (2000: 61). This is clearly important, but it is not the full story. As Angélil-Carter herself asserts (see chapter 12 in her book), there are other reasons when and why you should reference accurately in assignments.

Exercise: why reference?

In the space that follows write down the reasons **why** you think sources should be referenced in assignments:

8.2 Why reference?

You may have written one or more of the following reasons for why referencing is important in assignments:

1 To support your arguments and give credibility to the information presented.
2 To enable your tutors and other interested readers to trace the sources you cite and to use the same evidence for their own purposes.
3 To enable tutors and others to check the accuracy and validity of the evidence you have presented.
4 To help you trace the origin of ideas. You may want to find out who has influenced particular writers, and how the ideas presented by them have developed and been influenced by other authors.
5 To help to build a 'web' of connected ideas in an assignment. You can show a connection of ideas between writers, but also indicate the differences among them.
6 To help your tutors identify which authors or sources have been influential in shaping the direction taken by you in your assignment.
7 To give an appreciation to originators of work for their contribution to knowledge.
8 To avoid plagiarism.

I will argue, too, (in Chapter 10) that referencing is an essential part of helping you to find your 'own voice' in assignments.

Exercise: When to reference?

Look at the following situations that can occur when writing assignments and decide if a reference is needed at that point in the assignment:

Situation	Yes	No
1 When quoting directly from a source.		
2 To show the source of any statistics or other data.		
3 When summarizing what has happened over a period of time, and where there is general agreement by commentators on cause and effect.		
4 When using definitions available freely in the public domain, e.g. from websites.		

Situation	Yes	No
5 When summarizing or paraphrasing what is found on a website, and when no writer, editor, or author name is shown.		
6 When summarizing or paraphrasing what a particular writer or commentator has said on a topic.		
7 When summarizing, e.g. in a concluding section or paragraph, what has been discussed and referenced earlier in your text.		
8 To show the source of photographs freely available on the Internet and where no named photographer is mentioned.		
9 When using information supplied by your tutor in a course handout.		
10 When stating freely available facts in the public domain about or relevant to a topic.		

Now look at Appendix 6 for answers and comments.

8.3 When to reference

I have suggested elsewhere (Neville 2007) that you should present your sources of evidence in assignments in the following situations, some of which inevitably overlap with the 'why' of referencing.

1 To give the reader the source of tables, photos, statistics, and diagrams included in your assignment. These may be items directly copied, or which have been a source of collation for you.
2 When describing or discussing a theory, model, or practice associated with a particular writer. This would include the names of authors who coined words to label particular phenomena or situations.
3 To give weight or credibility to an argument presented by you, or supported by you, in your assignment.
4 When giving emphasis to a particular idea that has found a measure of agreement and support amongst commentators.
5 To inform the reader of sources of direct quotations or definitions in your assignment.
6 When paraphrasing another person's idea that you feel is particularly significant or likely to be a subject of debate; this can include sources of definitions you use in assignments.

8.4 When you don't need to reference

You don't need to reference, however, when;

1 Information is drawn from a variety of sources to summarize what has happened over a period of time and when the summary is unlikely to be a cause of dispute or controversy. However, if you use just one source for your summary, this should be cited and referenced.
2 When pulling together, in your conclusion, a range of key ideas that you introduced and referenced earlier in the assignment.
3 Your own experiences are cited, unless these have been published, in which case you can reference your own work.
4 When stating or summarizing what is generally regarded as 'common knowledge', which relates to generally undisputed facts, commonplace observations, or aphorisms circulating freely in the public domain, and when there is unlikely to be any significant disagreement with your statements or summaries of this knowledge.

But if in doubt, **always** reference your sources.

8.5 Avoiding plagiarism

To plagiarize means to deliberately take and use another person's **work** that has been presented in the public domain in some way and to claim it, directly or indirectly, as your own. 'Work' is usually something that has been produced by another person, 'published' in some tangible way, and presented formally into the public domain. This work can included printed texts, Internet and audio-visual sources, and theatrical, cinematic, choreographic, or other tangible production forms. It can also include assignments already written, or written to order, and sold from Internet sites, which are then presented to an institution by the buyer as his or her own original work.

The British media likes a good 'plagiarism story'. The activities within higher education are rarely of interest to the press because mostly good things happen there – and so, therefore, are 'not newsworthy'. However, plagiarism is news, and if you have read British newspapers over the last five years or so, you might have concluded that students generally are a devious, cheating lot, and that plagiarism is rife. Some students are devious and inclined to cheat, but probably only in the same proportion to their numbers as in any other group, including writers, politicians, and rat-catchers.

Many academics would say – although it is impossible to know the exact figures – that incidences of plagiarism have increased within higher education in Britain over the last ten years. This would appear to be associated with:

- Increasing numbers of students studying within higher education – more people studying is likely to increase the incidences of plagiarism.
- Convenient and quick access to the means of plagiarism: the Internet.
- Software, such as Turnitin, that help academics detect copy-and-paste forms of plagiarism more easily, so more incidences of plagiarism are coming to light.
- The pressure on students to succeed, linked with the high costs of learning. All students want to see a guaranteed return on their 'investment', and a minority will resort to plagiarism to do this.

But plagiarism, in my view, is not 'rife'. It is not rife because students, by and large, are still motivated to study for reasons linked to their search for self-respect, and for their future life and career prospects.

Self-respect, for many students, is linked with finding their 'own voice' in assessed work (see Chapter 10). For the individual, this means reading and discussing the work of others, but then presenting, summarizing, or paraphrasing it in **your** own way. It can also mean deciding where you stand, what **you** think, and what **your** conclusions are on a set topic. However, plagiarism gets in the way of this process. It is the equivalent of you allowing someone else to speak for you. It might seem like the easy option, but it does not lead to self-confidence – or self-respect. Most students know and understand this.

Most students, too, want to get a good job on the strength of their degree. Blatant plagiarism under the noses of tutors might get plagiarists a pass grade for this or that module, but the chances of them getting a decent set of grades consistently over the years are pretty remote if they plagiarize on a regular basis. Actions have consequences and perpetrators get caught out sooner or later – and when they do their grades suffer, along with their career chances.

How will you get caught out? A year or so ago I taught a module that attracted 120 students. The students submitted a portfolio of work. Most worked hard to produce individual work. But amongst these I spotted a handful of students who had obviously cut and pasted great chunks of someone else's work into their assignment. In one paragraph they clearly wrote in their own voice – but in the next the writing style changed radically, alerting me to the probability of plagiarism. It was then a simple enough matter for me to identify the source of this cut-and-paste job – the Internet. These few blatant examples of plagiarism were easily spotted, but there were other instances of 'grey plagiarism', where poor referencing practice had lead the students close to plagiarism territory. This tended to be where summaries of key sources had not been correctly cited in the text, or referenced fully in the list of references at the end of the assignment. Tutors want to see your expertise in both areas of referencing practice: the 'when' and the 'how' aspects of it. They will want to see that you understand when you need to acknowledge your sources, and that you have taken the trouble to learn how to do it in a consistent way.

Exercise: which of these scenarios would be regarded as plagiarism?

	Yes	No
1 There is a set of statistics on a freely available government website. You use them in your assignment, but forget to include the source in your references.		
2 You see a useful article on an Internet site. You copy 50 percent of the words and add 50 percent in your own words. You don't include a source, as no author's name is shown on the site.		
3 You find an interesting black and white illustration on a website. You copy and paste it into your assignment and don't include the designer or artist's name, as none is shown on the site.		
4 You are researching the impact of an historical event. You want to write a paragraph on what actually happened to include as background material in your assignment. You look at three reference books and they all say much the same thing on the cause of the problem. You summarize this in your own words, but do not reference the books you consulted.		
5 You find a definition of a concept on an Internet site encyclopedia, collaboratively written by its readers (a 'Wiki' site), which you use in your assignment. You do not reference this.		
6 You copy something from a course handout given to you by your tutor that contains secondary source information, i.e. the tutor has summarized the work of others. You do not reference this.		
7 You are part of a study group of six. You pair up and each pair agrees to write a third of the assignment and then pool the work. All the members of the group then submit the collated assignment individually.		
8 You include the expression, 'Children should be seen and not heard', in your essay without a source reference.		
9 You have a conversation with a classmate about an essay assignment. She or he has an interesting perspective on the topic, which makes you think. You decide to use this idea; no reference is included in your essay.		
10 You have been told that your assignment essay must be 'all your own work'. However, you are worried about your spelling and grammar so you pay a proofreader to check your work. The proofreader suggests changes to sentences throughout the essay to help the meaning becoming clearer to a reader. You accept these changes and submit the assignment.		

Now look at Appendix 6 for answers and comments on this exercise.

8.6 How to reference

Learning to reference correctly is your best way to avoid plagiarism. But many students can find the technical process difficult. What difficulties have you encountered so far with the technical 'how to' aspects of referencing? Do your difficulties connect with one or more of those listed next? If so, tick which.

Exercise: Common problems of referencing

- Citing and referencing secondary sources, particularly where author B refers to the work of author A – which is the information that interests you. □
- Presenting separate lists of sources, e.g. books, journals, or websites, instead of one alphabetical list (relating to Harvard, APA, and MLA referencing styles – see later in this chapter). □
- Not listing sources in alphabetical order within references or bibliographies (relating to Harvard, APA, and MLA referencing styles – see later in this chapter). □
- Missing vital information from a source listed in the references or bibliography, for example only supplying a URL website address in the list of references without the necessary additional information. □
- Citing sources in the text, but then not listing the source in the list of references or bibliography, or vice versa. □
- Not connecting citation information accurately to sources listed in the references or bibliography, e.g. name cited in text does not accord with the source detail listed in the full reference. □
- Giving too much information in an intext citation. □
- Not recognizing surnames from forenames in a list of references or bibliography. □

Exercise: Getting to grips with referencing style

The main way to overcome problems with the 'how to' aspects of referencing is to understand and manage the referencing style adopted by your institution or faculty. But do you know which referencing style has been adopted?

There are nine referencing styles found within Britain, although these fall broadly within two main categories: name and number related. Tick which referencing style(s) you are expected to use on your course:

In-text name referencing styles:
Harvard (author–year) style ☐   **APA** (author–year) style ☐   **MLA** (author–page) style ☐
Numerical referencing styles:
Running notes (footnotes) style ☐   **OSCOLA** (footnotes) style (for Law students) ☐   **MHRA** (footnotes) style ☐   **Numeric** (bracketed number) style ☐   **Vancouver** (bracketed number) style) ☐   **IEEE** (bracketed number) style ☐

Although all nine referencing styles can be found within higher education in Britain, they are incorporated into four broad styles, as follows.

8.6.1 Author–year styles (Harvard and APA)

Both these styles require you to cite in the text of your assignment the name(s) of author(s) or organization with year of publication. All sources are listed alphabetically at the end of an assignment and labelled 'References' or 'Bibliography'. There are relatively small differences between Harvard and APA style, and the main noticeable differences tend to be with citation punctuation, the way multiple authors are cited and referenced, and with the ways electronic sources are cited and referenced.

8.6.2 Author–page style (MLA)

This differs from Harvard and APA in that the page number, instead of year of publication, is cited in the text, e.g. (Handy 149). The full list of references at the end of the text is also labelled 'Works Cited' or 'Works Consulted'.

Proper words in the titles of works cited are capitalized and underlined. The last name of an author is followed by the full first name(s), for example:

> Handy, Charles. *Beyond Certainty: The Changing Worlds of Organisations*. *London: Hutchinson, 1995*.

The second line onwards in the full reference is also indented by five points, as shown in the example above.

8.6.3 Running notes style

This style uses superscript (or bracketed numbers) in the text, which connect with a reference in either footnotes or chapter endnotes. A bibliography is included at the end of the assignment, which lists alphabetically all the works referred to in the notes. This system uses a different number for each reference in the text.

8.6.4 Numeric style

This style uses bracketed (or superscript) numbers in the text that connect with a list of references at the end of the text. The same number can recur, e.g. if a source is mentioned more than once in the text.

It is not the intention of this chapter to go into detailed information about referencing styles, but to highlight that there are differences in the way that sources are presented, and to encourage you to learn the correct ways to reference your sources within the styles adopted by your institutions. Here are some examples of referencing in action for each of the four main groups of referencing styles, but a list of recommended texts is shown at the end of the chapter.

Example: Harvard and APA styles

As stated earlier, Harvard and APA styles use the names of authors or originators in the text, along with the date of publication. You would show the source of evidence in your assignment by giving (or citing) a **shortened** reference. This means you would cite the last name or names of the writers, or the name of something, e.g. organization, website, institution etc, with the date of publication. The following extract from an essay gives examples of three citations (shown in bold).

Advertising to children has therefore emerged as a topic of debate, especially during the past 25 years. At first the debate focused on the extent of children's understanding of the advertising message, and secondly there was a notion that children may not comprehend the persuasive aspect of advertising, with fears being voiced that children are therefore unable to defend against advertising. **Macklin and Carlson (1999)** argue that such concerns have been heightened by the increase in spending to capture the children's market. **Crowe (1997)** has estimated that the US television advertising directed to children cost US$894 million during 1996. Advertisers have been willing to spend large amounts of money because they realize that the children's market is huge. **McNeal (1998)** estimated that children under 14 years spent US$24 billion in direct purchases and influenced family spending by another US$188 billion during 1997.

Example: MLA style

The essential difference between the author date (Harvard and APA) style and the MLA referencing style is that with MLA, instead of the publication year, the page number(s) is used instead. For example, in the same essay extract, it would look like this:

> Advertising to children has therefore emerged as a topic of debate, especially during the past 25 years. At first the debate focused on the extent of children's understanding of the advertising message, and secondly there was a notion that children may not comprehend the persuasive aspect of advertising, with fears being voiced that children are therefore unable to defend against advertising. **Macklin and Carlson (59)** argue that such concerns have been heightened by the increase in spending to capture the children's market. **Crowe (47)** has estimated that the US television advertising directed to children cost US$894 million during 1996. Advertisers have been willing to spend large amounts of money because they realize that the children's market is huge. **McNeal (38)** estimated that children under 14 years spent US$24 billion in direct purchases and influenced family spending by another US$188 billion during 1997.

At the end of your assignment you then give full details of the source in a list headed either 'References' or 'Bibliography' (or in the case of MLA style 'Works Cited' or 'Works Consulted'.

8.7 What's the difference between references and a bibliography?

- A **bibliography** is a list of everything you have read in preparation for the assignment, whether or not you referred to it in your writing.
- **References** are the items you have read and referred to in your assignment. Some tutors like you to include both references and a bibliography; others prefer you to just include references. You need, therefore, to check this out with your tutor.

For Harvard, APA, and MLA styles, you list your sources in full in **alphabetical order** at the end of the assignment in one list. You do not subdivide this list, according to the type of source; there is just one continuous and alphabetical list presented. There are, however, some differences stylistically in the way these are shown for each referencing style. Assuming you only used just these three sources, they would be listed, as follows:

Example: Harvard referencing style – full reference details

CROWE, B. (1997). Advertisers see big guys in little eyes. *Broadcasting and Cable Journal*, July 28, p.47.
MACKLIN, M.C., and L. CARLSON. (Eds.) (1999). *Advertising to Children: Concepts and Controversies*. Thousand Oaks, CA: Sage.
McNEAL, J. (1998). Tapping the three kids' markets. *American Demographics*, April, No. 20, pp: 36–41.

Example: APA referencing style – full reference details

Crowe, B. (1997). Advertisers see big guys in little eyes. *Broadcasting and Cable Journal*, July 28, 47.
Macklin, M.C. & Carlson. L. (Eds.) (1999). *Advertising to children: Concepts and controversies*. Thousand Oaks, CA: Sage.
McNeal, J. (1998). Tapping the three kids' markets. *American Demographics*, April, 20, 36–41.

Items one and three above are journal articles; item two is an edited book. Note the relatively small differences between the two styles, including the indentation necessary in the APA style if the reference goes over one line in length, the use of ampersands (&) in place of 'and', and the position of the initial of the second author's first name.

Example: MLA referencing style – full reference details

There are more noticeable differences between the MLA and Harvard and APA styles in the way sources are presented. Note, for example, that the first name of the author is shown in full, following the surname; that titles are underlined; that the year of publication is shown toward the end of the reference; and how the second line is indented.

Crowe, Bill. 'Advertisers See Big Guys in Little Eyes'. *Broadcasting and Cable Journal*, July 28, (1997): 47.
Macklin, M. Carole and Les Carlson, Eds. *Advertising to Children: Concepts and Controversies*. Thousand Oaks, CA: Sage, 1999.
McNeal, James. 'Tapping the three kids' markets'. *American Demographics*, April 20, (1998) 36–41.

Example: Running notes referencing style (British Standard)

As stated earlier, this style uses superscript (or bracketed numbers) in the text. This system uses a different number for each note or reference in the text each time it is cited. One source may have many different numbers attached to it, depending on how often it is cited in the assignment. These numbers connect with citations at the bottom of the page (footnotes), or at the end of the assignment, headed 'Endnotes' or 'Notes'. The full reference details of sources are shown against the numbers in the numerical order they appear in your assignment. Using this style, the essay shown earlier would look like this:

Advertising to children has therefore emerged as a topic of debate, especially during the past 25 years. At first the debate focused on the extent of children's understanding of the advertising message, and secondly there was a notion that children may not comprehend the persuasive aspect of advertising, with fears being voiced that children are therefore unable to defend against advertising. Macklin and Carlson[1] argue that such concerns have been heightened by the increase in spending to capture the children's market. It has been estimated that the US television advertising directed to children cost US$894 million during 1996[2]. Advertisers have been willing to spend large amounts of money because they realize that the children's market is huge. McNeal[3] estimated that children under 14 years spent US$24 billion in direct purchases and influenced family spending by another US$188 billion during 1997.

[1] MACKLIN, M.C., and L. CARLSON. (Eds.) *Advertising to Children: Concepts and Controversies.* Thousand Oaks, CA: Sage, 1998.
[2] CROWE, B. Advertisers see big guys in little eyes. *Broadcasting and Cable Journal*, July 28, p.47, 1997.
[3] Mc NEAL, J. Tapping the three kids' markets. *American Demographics*, April 20, pp:36–41, 1998.

Example: Abbreviations

Because this referencing style uses a different number for each source in the text, to save you needing to repeat the same full reference information in your footnotes or endnotes, you can use abbreviations to link the references:

- **ibid.** (*ibidem*) meaning: in the same book, chapter, passage etc. and in the previous reference. If used, you should always give the relevant page numbers.
- **op. cit.** (*opere citato*) meaning: in the work quoted. This is used for a further reference to a source previously cited, but not the one immediately preceding it. If you use it, give some means of identifying the previous reference, such as author's name and date of publication.

- **loc. cit.** (*loco citato*) meaning: in the same place in a work previously cited, i.e. a reference to the same work, the same volume, or same page.

---

3. Mc NEAL, J. Tapping the three kids' markets. *American Demographics*, April 20, pp:36–41, 1998.
4. ibid. p. 36.

The two subdivisions of the running notes style: OSCOLA (Legal) style and MHRA style, follow the basic approach outlined here, but there are differences in the ways that the full reference details are presented.

Example: The numeric referencing style

The Numeric referencing style uses a bracketed (or superscript) number in the text, which connects with a list of references at the end of the text. If brackets are used to enclose numbers, you can use either square [ ] or curved () brackets, but make sure you are consistent. The same number can be repeated, for example, if a source is mentioned more than once in the same assignment, and this differentiates this style from running notes. The numbers connect with the same number in your final list of references.

The advantage of the numeric referencing style is that only one number is used **per source** and there is no need to use abbreviations (e.g. ibid. op. cit or loc. cit.), as is the case with the running notes style. If you want to refer to the same source on a number of occasions in the same assignment, but to different pages, you can add the relevant page numbers to the bracketed source reference numbers, e.g. (3: 42) or (3: 42–47).

The two subdivisions of the running notes style (Vancouver and IEEE style) follow the basic approach outlined here, but there are differences in the ways that the full reference details are presented.

8.7.1 Further reading

For more detailed information on specific referencing styles see:

1 **APA referencing style**. APA (American Psychological Association) (2005) *Concise Rules of APA Style*. Washington, DC: APA.
2 **Harvard referencing style:** BS (British Standard Institution) (1990) *Recommendations for Citing and Referencing Published Material*, BS 5605. London: BS.
3 **IEEE referencing style**: Institute of Electrical and Electronics Engineers (2006) *Transactions, Journals, and Letters: Information for Author*. Available at: http://standards.ieee.org/guides/style/section7.html (accessed 20 Jan. 2008).

4 **Legal referencing**: *Oxford Standard for Citation of Legal Authorities* (2005) www.competition-law.ox.ac.uk/published/oscola.shtml (accessed 20 Jan. 2008).
French, D. (1996) *How to Cite Legal Authorities*. London: Blackstone.
5 **MLA referencing style**: Gibaldi, J. (2003) *The MLA Handbook for Writers*. New York: Modern Language Association of America.
6 **MHRA referencing style**: Modern Humanities Research Association (2002). *A Handbook for Authors, Editors, and Writers of Thesis*. London: Modern Humanities Research Association
7 **Numeric and running notes (British Standard) referencing styles**: BS (British Standard Institution) (1990) *Recommendations for Citing and Referencing Published Material*, BS 5605. London: BS.
8 **Vancouver numeric referencing style**: ICMJE (International Committee of Medical Journal Editors) (2006) *Uniform Requirements for Manuscripts Submitted to Biomedical Journals: Sample References*. Available at: www.icmje.org/ (Accessed 14 Jan. 2008).

For general overview of referencing, with examples of different styles, see:

Neville, C. (2007) *The Complete Guide to Referencing and Avoiding Plagiarism*. Maidenhead: McGraw Hill/The Open University.
Pears, R. and Shields, G. (2005) *Cite Them Right: The Essential Guide to Referencing and Plagiarism*. Newcastle upon Tyne: Pear Tree Books.

Main points from this chapter:

• Accurate referencing is an essential part of the process of demonstrating and presenting knowledge in assignments.
• Not all sources need to be referenced; facts regarded as common knowledge, for example, do not need be referenced. **But if in doubt, always reference your sources**.
• There are nine referencing styles found within higher education in Britain, and each has its own conventions for citing and listing sources. You need to learn how to apply the style adopted by your institution, course, or faculty.
• Poor referencing practice can lead to accusations of plagiarism.
• The Internet makes plagiarism easy – but also easy to detect.

9

'Your English is weak: it was difficult to follow your arguments'

The price of mistakes • Comma confusion • Correct use of the apostrophe • Common errors • Spelling • Keep it short • The importance of redrafting and proofreading • Recommended reading

---

This chapter is about:

- The correct use of the apostrophe, comma, colon, and semicolon.
- The value of brevity in writing.
- Identifying commonly confused or misspelt words.
- The importance of proofreading your assignments.

Grammatical errors, poor spelling, and long confusing sentences can interrupt the process of communication between you and your tutor. If an essay or report is hard to follow or understand, it makes it difficult for a tutor to follow and understand your line of thought. This can cost you marks.

In one chapter of a book it is impossible to cover all these issues in an in depth way. However, a range of exercises is included for you to test your knowledge of writing skills, but if you feel you need to read more on the topic, please refer to the recommended reading list at the end of the chapter.

9.1 The price of mistakes

Grammatical errors and spelling mistakes can lose you marks – and job opportunities too, as employers are increasingly conscious of the economic costs to their businesses from communication errors made by their employees. A spelling or grammatical error, for example in an advertising or directional sign, is expensive to remedy, exposes a business to public ridicule, and can lead to loss of public trust.

For example, research carried out by Royal Mail in 2003 with 1000 customers suggested that three-quarters of the people surveyed did not trust businesses that made errors of spelling and grammar in marketing or other communications, and 30 percent said they would not do business with companies that made these mistakes (Royal Mail Group 2003).

The quality of English in job applications has also been the subject of critical attention in recent years. For example, a survey for the BBC in 2006 of 266 organizations, conducted by the Recruitment and Employment Federation (REF), concluded that almost half of all job applications (47 percent), contained basic grammatical and spelling mistakes. Applicants aged between 21 and 25 were found to have made the most mistakes, and men were worse than women. Common mistakes included misspelling 'curriculum vitae', 'liaison', and 'personal', and other errors included misplaced apostrophes and poor sentence construction (Plain English Campaign 2007). These mistakes give employers, faced with a large response to an advertised vacancy, the excuse to immediately bin those applications that contain spelling or grammatical errors.

Exercise: what's wrong with these sentences?

In the exercise that follows there are 12 punctuation errors. How many can you spot?

---

1 The University of XYZ is holding it's first 'Plagiarism Awareness Week' in February (13th–17th).
2 Its estimated that more than a thousand people were affected by the flood.
3 The CV's were'nt particularly impressive I'm afraid.
4 The report was succinct short and to the point.
5 The decision to introduce a new accounting system has already been made by the Director's.
6 I decided not to take out the insurance policy on principle because its too expensive.
7 I have devised a plan to ensure our place in the top ten SME's in the region.
8 The BBCs response to the MPs criticism was to invite the MPs to take part in a televized broadcast on the topic.

Look at Appendix 7 for the answers.

9.2 Comma confusion

The use or misuse of the comma is a common problem in student assignments. It is such an insignificant mark on the page, but the lack of a comma in the right place can change the meaning of a sentence. Take this sentence, for example:

> The Team Leader said Joe Brown was entirely to blame for the team's dismal performance.

This sentence suggests that the Team Leader was putting the blame on Joe Brown; the emphasis is put on what the Team Leader said: that Brown was entirely to blame.

However, addition of two commas can completely change the meaning:

> The Team Leader, said Joe Brown, was entirely to blame for the team's dismal performance.

The commas now change the emphasis to what Brown said about the Team Leader: that the Team Leader was to blame, not him!

Another example of changing the meaning of a sentence is:

> Woman without her man is nothing.

The meaning changes dramatically with some additional punctuation:

> Woman! Without her, man is nothing.

9.2.1 When to use commas

Rule	Example
1 To separate the clauses in a sentence.	Society depends on its traditions, and the authority of the written text is one of these.

Rule	Example
2 To separate the introductory element of a sentence from the main part (or subject) of it.	After the death of his wife, Hardy went into a deep depression.
3 To separate an additional and final part of a sentence from the opening and main part (or subject) of it.	The sea is calm tonight, yet it raged fiercely all day.
4 To separate out nonessential words from the remainder of the sentence. The word 'however' is used as a signal to suggest a change of direction or to stress an exception to the rule.	(a) There is, however, one mistake that many students make . . .
5 To separate out essential/useful information from the main part (subject) of the sentence	Charles Handy, in his book *The Empty Raincoat*, has argued that federalism is a way of making sense of large organizations.
6 To separate commands or interjections from the remainder of the sentence.	Stop, or I'll shoot. No, you are wrong. Yes, you are right. Phew, it's a hot day today.
7 To separate out (a) adjectives, or (b) list of items in a sentence.	(a) It was a fine, dry, and sunny day in my home town. (b) Raspberries, strawberries, blackberries, and gooseberries are all traditional English summer fruits.

9.3 Correct use of the apostrophe

The apostrophe is used in the following situations:

1 To show where a letter(s) or figures have been left out

Examples:

- 'It is' can be merged to **it's**.
- 'You will' can be merged to **you'll**.
- 'He is' can be merged to **he's**.
- 'Do not' can be merged to **don't**.
- 2008 can be merged, if appropriate, to **'08**.

However, whilst using an apostrophe is acceptable for informal writing that imitates conversational speech, it should be avoided in formal writing for assignment purposes.

2 **To indicate possession**
This is when the apostrophe shows ownership or possession of something by someone or something.
Examples:
• The University's Charter • The Universities' Charters • The course's aims • The module's outcomes • The School's Mission Statement. • Women's rights. • The tutors' salaries.

9.4 Common errors

- **It's and its**: it is (or it's) easy to confuse the use of these two.
- **It's**: only used when a letter has been left out, e.g. 'It's (it is) nearly time to go'; 'It's (it is) a hot day today'.
- **Its**: no apostrophe is used when the word is used to denote possession, for example, the 'School opened its new library today'; or, 'the company closed its account with the bank this week; or, 'the University launches its new Mission Statement this month'.

9.4.1 Plural problems

Apostrophes are never used to denote plurals. For example:

- A sign at a railway station, 'Taxi's only', contains a grammatical mistake, as it is referring to taxis in the plural, not something belonging to a taxi.
- The words 'CD's, Video's, Book's and Gift's' should not contain apostrophes when they refer to these items in the plural.
- Another common mistake is to add an apostrophe to CV's; it should be CVs, if denoting plural.

9.4.2 Should the apostrophe come before or after the 's'?

A useful way of helping you to resolve this question is to change the phrase around so that the word before the apostrophe is placed last. If it still has the same meaning, the apostrophe was correct. For example:

- The **boy**'s books: the books belonging to the **boy**.
- The **boys**' books: the books belonging to the **boys**.
- The **children**'s books: the books belonging to the **children**.
- **Men**'s shirts: shirts belonging to the **men**.

but:

- **Peoples**' wishes: wishes of the **peoples** (wrong).
- **People**'s wishes: wishes of the **people** (correct).

9.5 Spelling

Spell-checkers on personal computers will highlight many obvious spelling errors, but they have their limitations. They cannot assume or tell how you are using a particular word and often will be confused by both correctly and incorrectly spelt proper nouns. You also need to ensure your computer is set to recognize spelling errors in English (UK), rather than English (US), as standard British spelling differs from American for some words; for example, showing English (UK) first in each pair: colour/color; labour/labor; centre/center; judgement/judgment.

Exercise

Here is a selection of words that can confuse a spell-checker. The most common interpretations of the words are shown in brackets. Some examples are left blank for you to write the respective meanings in the spaces.

Accept: to take from	Except: to leave out
Affect:	Effect:
Allowed: permitted	Aloud: spoken
Altar: raised area for worship	Alter: to change
Ascent:	Assent
Band: a musical group	Banned: forbidden
Bear: an animal	Bare: naked
Board: a plank, or group (Board)	Bored: not interested

Brake: stopping device	Break: to damage
Buy: purchase	By: near; of
Cited:	Sited:
Complement:	Compliment:
Fair: even-handed	Fare: price of
Miner: coal worker	Minor: small
Ordinance:	Ordnance:
Passed: moved on	Past: before now; history
Praise: commend	Preys: hunts
Precedence:	Precedents:
Principal:	Principle:
Stationery:	Stationary
Summary: précis	Summery: of the summer
Their: possessive pronoun, e.g. their toys	There: relating to place
To: indicating movement towards	Too: also
Weather: meteorological condition	Whether: if it be the case
Your: possessive pronoun, e.g. your car	You're: contraction for 'you are'

Look at Appendix 8 for answers.

9.6 Keep it short

Another important element in effective writing is brevity. 'A sentence is more likely to be clear if it is a short sentence communicating one thought, or a closely connected range of ideas' (Evans 2000: 17). Effective writing will contain a mixture of sentence types and sentence lengths, which gives rhythm, pace, and variety to writing. However, overlong sentences risk confusing or boring the reader if they have to navigate a mass of information. To write effective 30+ word sentences requires a firm grasp of grammar, so that the main idea and modifying clauses in the sentence are made clear to the reader. In particular, knowing when and how to use the colon and the semicolon correctly is important to help you manage long sentences and to give your writing more authority.

The colon (:) can be used in the latter part of a sentence to signal that there is more to come. It may substitute for expressions such as:

- 'Namely . . .'
- 'In other words . . .'
- 'For instance . . .'
- 'For example . . .'
- 'On the other hand . . .'
- In particular . . .

It can also introduce lists, start off quotations, separate the main from subtitles in texts, and separate the dialogue from a character's name in a play.

Example: uses of the colon

As he grew older Joseph found he became more paranoid in two main ways: his dislike of spending his own money, and his dislike of others spending his money.

The way ahead for the organization was quite clear: to reorganize, regroup, and rethink their strategy.

There was no substitute: it had to be Brand X.

Other factors included: rising costs of fuel and feed, labour costs, and the demographic changes in the region.

Harris became famous for his slogan: 'never say never, ever.'

The backlog in orders continued to build. One person familiar with the system likened it to a sponge: 'It could take so much water and then no more'

The semicolon (;) is used to link two related sentences, where the use of full stops or conjunctions, such as 'and' would lead to jerky or ungrammatical prose. It is also used to differentiate and separate items in a list.

Example: uses of the semicolon

Creativity has often been suppressed within adults by the conventions and routines of everyday life; but it is still there and can be reawakened.

The communication of this strategy to the satellite companies involved a great number of slogans: 'continuous improvement'; 'benchmarking'; 'learning organization'; 'common approach'; and 'we're in it for the long haul'.

At first the purpose seemed to be clear; however, this soon changed.

9.6.1 The word count challenge

Writing within the set word count for assignments is one of the biggest challenges that students face, and many find it very difficult to confine their essays within a set word limit. However, this is all part of the discipline of academic writing and by eliminating unnecessary words your writing becomes sharper and makes more impact. Look at the following introduction to an essay.

Example: essay introduction

Before embarking on an approach to analyse the business model there is a need to explore the meaning of the business model. Paul Timmers (2000) has defined the business model as 'an architecture for product, service and information flows, including a description of the various business actors and their roles' (p.32). Although there are different kinds of business model they have got one thing in common and that is they are designed to make money for their owners in the long run.

There are 82 words in this extract. But the extract can be reduced by a quarter without loss of meaning. Alternative words can be substituted for those cut, and the grammar changed. The emboldened sections in both columns show you where changes have been made:

Before	After
Before **embarking on an approach to** analyse the business model there is a need to explore **the meaning of the business model**. **Paul** Timmers (2000) **has** defined the business model as 'an architecture for product, service and information flows, including a description of the various business actors and their roles' (p.32). Although there are different **kinds of** business model they have **got** one thing in common **and that is** they are designed to make money for their owners **in the long run**. (82 words)	Before **analysing** the business model, there is a need to explore **its** meaning. Timmers (2000) defined the business model as 'an architecture for product, service and information flows, including a description of the various business actors and their roles' (p.32). Although there are different business models, they have one thing in common: they are designed to make money for their owners. (61 words)

Note the use of the colon in the second paragraph of the amended version. The word count in assignments can be managed by pruning unnecessary words, or even sentences, from your paragraphs; like shrubs, it does them good! Try and substitute multiple words with one wherever possible. Here are a few examples:

Multiple words	Alternative word
Ahead of schedule	Early
A large proportion of	Many
Despite the fact that . . .	Although
Give consideration to	Consider
In many cases	Often
Made an approach to	Approached
One of the purposes	One purpose

It is not that the words on the left are necessarily wrong, but the alternatives are shorter, which can help cut down on the assignment word count. The alternatives are also more direct.

In the following example the student has attempted to clarify terms, cut redundant words, and review the punctuation. The emboldened sections in both columns show you where changes have been made:

Before	After
Before discussing the advantages and disadvantages of 'inclusive' and 'exclusive' education, it is important to understand the historical **context of the notion and distinctions** of 'disability', 'special needs,' and 'special educational needs'. This will allow us to **picture the journey and the pace of change that has taken place to the very** contentious **political** issue of 'integrated' education **it is today. It will discuss the** competing perspectives behind inclusion and exclusivity **leading onto the discussion of** whether it is possible for integration to be applied to all children with SN or just children with SEN. (95 words)	Before discussing the advantages and disadvantages of 'inclusive' and 'exclusive' education, it is important to understand the historical context of 'disability', 'special needs,' and 'special educational needs'. This will allow us to understand the current contentious and politicised issue of 'integrated' education. This essay, therefore, discusses the competing perspectives behind inclusion and exclusivity and whether it is possible for integration to be applied to all children with SN, or just children with SEN. (73 words)

Exercise: reducing the word count

Here are three short exercises in word count reduction for you to try. Write in the blank right hand column of each example. Try to amend each paragraph that follows without losing its meaning. Aim to reduce the number of words in this first example by around half:

The dollar has been declining in value against the euro over the last six years, hurting travellers to Europe and American consumers purchasing European goods. The strengthening euro has not had the expected beneficial impact in Europe, as trade with North America has shown a downward trajectory as a result. (50 words)	

Again, in this second example, try to cut the number of words to around half without losing the meaning:

A new analysis of online consumer data (ComScore 2008) shows that large web companies are learning about the tastes and preferences of people from what they search for and do on the Internet. The data from the search engines of Internet users is routinely gathered and analysed and knowledge gained by the web companies about the things that users are most interested in. (62 words)	

In this third example try to cut as many words as you can without losing the meaning:

The public's knowledge of health is poor and more government funding for health education is needed. Increased sums of money should be spent on courses to make people aware of personal health issues. People don't always know what they can do to take care of their health, so further investment is needed in training on health matters. (57 words)	

Look at Appendix 7 for comments on these exercises.

9.7 The importance of redrafting and proofreading

Few writers can produce a final draft in just one attempt. Most have to write a first draft, leave it for a while, and then prepare a redraft. Proofreading is also a very important part of the process of checking your work before submission.

Proofreading includes checking a text for spelling mistakes and grammatical errors. Tutors, dissertation supervisors, or the staff of learning support units cannot proofread assignments or dissertations as it is a very time consuming process and requires particular skills. However, if you cannot find another student, friend, or relative willing to proofread your assignment, then learning support staff at your institution may be able to recommend a professional proofreader to you.

Professional proofreaders charge a fee for their services. They will always highlight technical errors, but will leave the final decision about changing the text to you. A professional proofreader will never attempt or persuade you to change your ideas or style of writing; and it is essential for you to retain 'ownership' of the assignment content and presentation.

This is important, because to avoid plagiarism the work should be your own ideas, written in your own words. However, a proofreader will point out spelling and grammatical errors. If you make a note of these, it can help you to develop your English and can be an important part of learning. There is certainly no shame in using a proofreader, as it is very easy to overlook spelling mistakes, common grammatical errors, and convoluted sentence constructions when writing under time pressure. This book will have gone through several layers of proofreading scrutiny before it gets to you, and even then errors can slip through; please let me know if you spot anything!

The Society for Editors and Proofreaders has an online and searchable directory, which contains information on skills (editing/proofreading/ indexing/ etc.) and subject areas, so you can find a proofreader with knowledge of your subject area. Their website is at: www.sfep.org.uk/pub/dir/ directory.asp

You can use search words to find members of the society that offer a proofreading service in your home area; their members operate under a code of conduct, which you can read on their website. Not all proofreaders are a member of the society, and if they are not, you should always check their qualifications and experience.

9.8 Recommended reading

If you feel you want or need to learn more on the topics raised in this chapter, the following books will take you a stage or two further:

Collinson, D. et al. (1992) *Plain English*. Buckingham: Open University Press.
Peck, J. and Coyle, M. (2005) *The Student's Guide to Writing: Grammar, Punctuation and Spelling*. Basingstoke: Palgrave MacMillan.
Sinclair, C. (2007) *Grammar: A Friendly Approach*. Maidenhead: Open University Press.
Truss, L. (2003) *Eats, Shoots & Leaves: The Zero Tolerance Approach to Punctuation*. London: Profile Books.

Main points from this chapter:

- Learn the rules for using commas and apostrophes correctly.
- Do not rely on spell-checkers; familiarize yourself with words pronounced alike, but spelled differently and with different meanings.
- Varied sentence lengths add interest to writing, but as a general rule try to keep your sentences short.
- Using colons and semicolons correctly can help you manage long sentences.
- Be ruthless and cut out any unnecessary words.
- Always proofread your assignments before submitting them.

10

Finding your own voice in assignments

Example essay • Commentary • Developing your own writing style • You and 'I'

This chapter is about:

- What it means to 'write in your own voice'.
- Analysing the elements of 'own voice' writing.
- The conventions of academic writing, and when to use first person terms in essays.

If you have fallen into a habit of copying and pasting bits of other people's work into your own assignments, what emerges is a babble of voices and not your own. Your tutor will sense this, you will know it, and, as a result, it is likely you will coast to a degree with an indifferent grade. It is also likely you will feel a sense of disappointment in your performance.

So what does 'finding your own voice in assignments' actually mean? It sounds like one of those woolly expressions much beloved of educationalists, but in fact it is quite simple. It means that you gain **ownership** of your own work by:

- Deciding **yourself** which position or direction to take in an assignment.
- Selecting evidence that allows **you** to present a strong set of arguments or descriptions.

- Summarizing or paraphrasing in **your** own words what you read.
- Writing in a style that comes from within.

Cut-and-paste approaches to writing assignments cause you to lose ownership of the work. If you didn't care about this, the chances are you wouldn't be reading this book – so read on.

The best way of illustrating the points I am making is to show you an essay written by a postgraduate student; it is on the topic of life change, so it should appeal to students from a range of disciplines as studying for a degree is a significant life change experience.

10.1 Example essay

This is an example essay that demonstrates how the student presents an individual point of view and reaches a particular conclusion, but does so in a seemingly objective way.

Exercise: before you read the essay

Look closely at the essay title and pick out any key words and assumptions and think about what you are being asked to do in the task.

Title
How have life transitions changed over the last three decades in Britain? What are the implications for individuals in managing transition and change in the future?

Key words	Assumptions

Then, as you read, I suggest you underline or mark any section you feel is:

- Descriptive, but then interprets what has been described.
- Central to the essay task.
- An example of the student writing in her own voice.

Also look at:

- The way the student manages evidence and think about why certain sections are not referenced.

And ask yourself:

- Has the student answered the question posed in the title and engaged with the set task?
- Would I write this essay differently, and if so, how and why?

The paragraphs are numbered to help with the commentary that follows, but normally assignments would not be numbered in this way.

Example: an essay

Title: How have life transitions changed over the last three decades in Britain? What are the implications for individuals in managing transition and change in the future? (Maximum 2000 words)

1   '*Things ain't what they used to be*' . . . so went the chorus to a popular song of the 1960s. But things have never been what they used to be: life is never static; there has always been change in society. However, the aggregate of economic change since the early 1970s has had a profound impact on the working lives of people in Britain, which in turn has affected other aspects of their lives. This essay will trace the rise of ideas that linked life transitions with 'predictable' age related stages, and how these ideas changed following the 1973 Oil Crisis. It will be argued that people now ask different questions about their present and future lives, compared to thirty years ago.

2   Transition and change: the terms are often used interchangeably and, indeed, there is a sense of both movement and alteration conveyed in both. However, the term 'transition', in the context of this essay, relates to the emotional processes that are involved in moving from one state of existence to another; whereas 'change' refers to the altered state itself. Bridges (2003) identifies three emotional phases of transition: 'letting go; passing through 'the neutral zone', when emotional realignments take place; and emergence into a new situation. Hopson et al (1993) also identify the movement element implicit in the word transition. They see it as a 'passage' that will last a certain period of time within which something happens: 'one style is developing into another' (p.11). So common within both these explanations is an overall sense that a transition is an emotional 'journey' of indeterminate length at the end of which change occurs.

3   For centuries life has been seen as a 'journey' through a series of stages. Virgil, in Ancient Greece, likened human life to the rise and fall of the seasons, and within the world's great religions we find the idea of life as a spiritual transitional journey in stages of spiritual growth and enlightenment. In the sixteenth century Shakespeare's view of life saw it proceeding through a series of seven stages, with maximum power reached at a broad 'middle passage' of life, from early to middle adulthood. But it was in the twentieth century, with the rise of psychology as a discipline, when the academic study of life span began in earnest and the idea of stages of life was developed in a formal, academic way. For example, Charlotte Buhler, a German psychologist, established an institute in Vienna to study human development; she proposed that the life course was a process in broadly three stages of physical, social and cognitive growth, followed by a period of stability, and then descent toward death (Buhler1935). Later in the century Erikson, in the 1950s, proposed a theory of human development that saw life advancing in eight steps, each one taking us higher to greater maturity and wisdom, and each preceded by 'turning points', or 'crisis' (Erikson 1959).

4   However, from the 1970s onwards the idea of life stages was developed further using the notion of specific age related developmental tasks. For example, in 1976 Gail Sheehy, building on Erikson's ideas, attempted to identify the personality changes common to people within a series of age stages. She suggested that there was an 'impulse to change' within all people: a type of built-in developmental and transitional urge to move on from one phase or stage of life to another. Reaching certain age stages gave impetus to these 'programmed' changes and, as she described them, the 'predictable crisis of adulthood' (Sheehy 1976).

5   The term 'crisis' also featured in Daniel Levinson's 1978 survey of forty middle-aged men (then later, in 1986, with forty-five middle aged women), which described four major periods of life, each overlapping with the other and each lasting about twenty-five years: childhood and adolescence; early adulthood; middle adulthood, and late adulthood. Each phase was characterised by calm periods of relative emotional stability, but these gave way to 'crisis', particularly in the period between phases. If these periods were navigated successfully, the self and the world fitted together in new, but satisfactory ways (Levinson et al 1978; Levinson 1986). Patricia Cross took this idea further and attempted to describe life cycle phases in a three-dimensional way. She divided life stages into age-marked phases, each phase characterised by 'physic tasks', 'marker events', and 'characteristic stances'. In the 29–34 life stage, for example, the psychic (intrinsic) tasks included a search for personal values, setting long-range goals, and a re-appraisal of relationships. Marker events typically included the birth of children; and the characteristic stance, or attitude, was in the form of career self-

questioning, a concern for order and stability in life affairs, and an increasing desire to set and meet long range goals (Cross 1981).

6   In summary, what the Sheehy, Levinson and Cross studies have in common is a way of separating life into stages marked by age bands, each age band marked by a need to play a particular role in the world; a role driven by two connected needs. There is an intrinsic need to develop and change, and then move on extrinsically in some way. Age plays a role of signalling or reminding us of the need for changes of direction. These 'signals' are given impetus by political forces that circumscribe individual changes, by for example, setting specific age limits to achieve particular economic purposes, i.e. fixed retirement age. This can result in a connection between individual identities and state economic needs based on what Estes, Biggs and Phillipson (2003) have described as 'relations of production' (p.35). It can be argued that a central thread to these 1970 and early 1980 age stage ideas is in an implicit assumption that life, particularly economic life, was relatively stable and predictable. Cross, for example, saw the age stage 45–55 as the 'settling down' phase when one could enjoy the fruits of steady labour. The next stage, described by Cross as 'the mellowing' phase, saw the person in 'preparation for retirement', displaying a 'mellowing of feelings and relationships', and experiencing 'greater comfort with self'.

7   There was also an explicit connection among these stage idea commentators between life and nature: a connection between the rhythms of life and the fixed patterns of the seasons. Levinson, for example, titled his book 'The Seasons of a Man's Life', and Sheehy refers to the life course in terms of nature metaphors: 'a stormy passage', and about 'pulling up and sending out new roots'. The assumption with all of this is that the life course, like the seasons, is predictable.

8   However, like the elements today – global warming being a good example – the interventionist hand of Man can change the predictable to the unpredictable. In particular, the Oil Crisis of 1973 provoked a significant global downturn in the economy and the resultant spiralling costs of energy forced manufacturing to reconsider their production and labour costs. Centres of manufacturing production shifted rapidly from the Western to the Eastern Hemisphere, where labour costs were cheaper, and the balance of the economy in the West moved from manufacturing to the service sector.

9   So out with the old in with the new, literally, as many older workers in all sectors of the economy, but particularly from manufacturing, began to be propelled into redundancy or cajoled into taking early retirement. The burgeoning service sector resulted in new, or more, career opportunities for women, but heralded a significant reduction of work opportunities for many men, particularly those from unskilled or semi-skilled work backgrounds. Unemployment became a significant feature of the economic scene in Europe from the late 1970s onward.

10 Long-term unemployment has badly affected men, particularly older (45+) men, and by 1999 in Britain nearly a quarter of unemployed men had been out of work for two or more years – and in one in four households the woman had become the main breadwinner (CSO 2000). Between 1990–1994, across Europe, the overall proportion of men (15–64 years) in employment fell from 81 per cent to 78 per cent, and by the mid 1990s a third of all men had withdrawn from the labour market by their late 50s (European Commission 1996).

11 Conversely, between 1971 and 2004 female employment in Britain rose from 42 to 70 per cent; this has had a profound impact on their lives, and in particular on their views of motherhood and relationships (WWC 2005). Career imperatives, combined with a rethink of individual preferences, led to a situation by 2000 where a quarter of UK women in their early 30s were unmarried, and 38 per cent childless, compared to 19 per cent thirty years earlier (CSO 2000). The traditional idea of abandonment of career at marriage, or when children arrive (if they do), is still an option today, but it is one among many.

12 The idea of a career for life, seen as a linear vertical progression within one major employing organization, has also gone for both men and women. What no longer exists is the concept of career, as implicit in the work of Sheehy, Levinson and Cross, where a different contractual relationship between employer and employee was marked by a sense of tenure, continuity and reciprocity. The former gave their loyalty and skill in exchange for security, increasing status, and financial reward from the employer. Paradoxically, despite the fact that nearly half of employees in Britain in 2000 had worked at least five years with the same employer (ONS 2001), workers feel now that they can no longer rely on their employing organizations to give them the security of long-term work tenure; conversely the employer wants the employee not to give life-long loyalty, but instead give the full range of their skills, flexibility and effort for as long as required (Burchell et al 1999).

13 Demographic changes too have had an impact on individual choices. The Employment Equality (Age) Regulations introduced in Britain in 2006 were a response to the fact that that nearly a third of the UK labour force will be over 50 by 2020. Employees cannot rely on a steady flow of younger people to fill gaps left by retired workers, and so employees can now negotiate with an employer about continuing to work beyond a normal retirement age. The legislation also gave a measure of protection to older people against being denied jobs or harassed because of their age and stipulates that, in most cases, workers of all ages should be given an equal chance of training and promotion.

14 The management of transition now includes decisions on a range of individualised issues and choices much less dependent on age stages. These choices can be said to mirror values inherent in a service sector dominated economy: the importance of 'choices', 'quality' (of life) and 'value for

money'. Questions individuals ask today about their futures focus on a broader range of life choice questions including: is a career to be the central perspective of my life or are there other preferences? Do I wish to remain single, co-habit, marry – and establish a family in any of these contexts? Will my future life planning be burdened by a property mortgage, or would I rather manage by renting? How will I live my life post 60 years?

15 A few decades ago these questions would have been rarely asked; now they are frequently asked by individuals, who see themselves with choices less circumscribed by age, gender, class or cultural stereotypes. Life choices have become more individualised and consumer choice driven. As we have seen, commentators could once comfortably describe 'typical' situations and could predict 'typical' futures. But we cannot do that any more.

References

BRIDGES, W. (2003). *Managing Transitions: Making the Most of Change.* London: Nicholas Brealey.

BUHLER, C. (1935). *From Birth to Maturity.* London: Kegan Paul, Trench, and Trubner.

BURCHELL, B.J. et al (1999). *Job Insecurity and Work Intensification: Flexibility and the Changing Boundaries of Work.* York: Joseph Rowntree Foundation.

CSO (Central Statistical Office) (2000) *Social Trends.* London: HMSO.

CROSS, P. (1981) *Adults as Learners.* Josey Bass.

ERIKSON, E. (1959). *Identity and the Life Cycle.* New York: International Universities Press.

ESTES, C. et al (2003). *Social Theory, Social Policy and Ageing: a Critical Introduction.* Maidenhead: Open University Press.

EUROPEAN COMMISSION (1996). *Employment in Europe.* HMSO

HOPSON, B. et al (1992). *Transitions: the Challenge of Change.* Didcot: Mercury.

KOTRE, J. and E. HALL (1990). *Seasons of Life: Our Dramatic Journey from Birth to Death.* Boston: Little, Brown and Co.

LEVINSON, D.J. et al (1978). *The Seasons of a Man's Life.* N.Y. Knopf.

LEVINSON, D.J. (1986). A conception of adult development. *American Psychologist* 41, pp. 3–13.

ONS: Office for National Statistics (2001). *Social Trends*, no.31. London: The Stationery Office.

SHEEHY, G. (1976) *Passages: Predictable Crises of Adult Life.* N.Y. Dutton.

WWC: WOMEN and WORK COMMISSION (2005). A fair deal for women in the workplace: an interim statement. [Report]. London: Government Equalities Office.

10.2 Commentary

We need to start with a close examination of the essay title:

> How have life transitions changed over the last three decades in Britain? What are the implications for individuals in managing transition and change in the future?

- This is a 'big' topic in that much has been written about it – and there is a 2000 word limit for the essay. The student has to choose from a large body of evidence and needs to consider if any particular historical catalyst in the 1970s or early 1980s might have given the pace of change a new trajectory.
- There are two parts to the question. There is an assumption that life transitions **have** changed, because the title is asking **how** have they changed? There is a specific period of time mentioned 'last three decades', which may suggest there is a pivotal period in the 1970s to consider.
- A discussion about what has happened recently is, however, only meaning-ful if it is put into a context of what happened in the past, so that com-parisons can be made. The essay title also presents two words 'transition' **and** 'change', suggesting there are conceptual differences between them.
- The title is also specific in mentioning the implications and responsibilities of 'individuals' in managing their own lives. It is important, therefore, that the essay distinguishes between these two concepts and keeps the focus in the second half of the essay on the implications for individuals rather than, say, for governments or employers.

The challenge, therefore, is to:

- Keep focused and engaged with both parts of the essay task.
- Define terms accurately, particularly distinguishing between 'transition' and 'change'.
- Select relevant and credible material to present a convincing case to justify the implications presented in part two of the essay.
- Resist copying and pasting from the myriad sources of information avail-able on the Internet and to write in one's 'own voice'.

10.2.1 Getting our attention: the introduction

The **introduction** starts with a line from a song, which gains our attention and makes a good lead in to the comment that there has always been change; life is not static. However, the student states that: 'it is the aggregate of economic change since the early 1970s that has impacted on the working lives of people in Britain over the last thirty years, which in turn has affected other spheres of life. This is an example of using 'own voice' early in the essay. It is a clear and definite statement and we look, therefore, for the student to justify this position with valid evidence. The structure of the essay is then outlined and the Oil Crisis of 1973 highlighted as a pivotal economic point in recent history. Another definite statement finishes the introduction: 'people now ask different questions about their present and future lives compared to thirty years ago'. Again, this is an intriguing statement that can arouse the curiosity and interest of the reader.

10.2.2 First half of the essay

In paragraph two definitions of 'transition' and 'change' are presented and the student has selected two main sources: William Bridges (2003) and Hopson et al. (1992), to support the points made. There are dozens of other sources the student could have chosen, but in a 2000 word essay you must pick selectively from the mainstream of commentators on the topic in question.

In paragraphs three to five, a brief historical overview is presented, which shows a development of life stage ideas. Again, there is a lot more that can be said on this, but the student must resist the temptation to pump out all he or she knows, in order to ensure a balance is achieved when addressing both parts of the essay title.

In paragraphs six and seven the essay moves from **description** and **summary** (paragraph six) to **interpretation** (paragraph seven) of the ideas summarized. This is important, as it shows the tutor that you understand the connections, assumption, and deeper significances of the ideas presented. The student writes, for example: 'There was also an explicit connection among these stage idea commentators between life and nature: a connection between the rhythms of life and the fixed patterns of the seasons' (paragraph 7). This came at about the half way mark in the essay, and we can see that this sentence forms an ideas 'bridge' between paragraphs seven and eight, in preparation for the shift from the first to the second half of the essay.

10.2.3 Second half of the essay

The word, 'however', at the start of paragraph eight is a 'signal' that alerts us to a change of direction, and in paragraphs eight and nine we have a brief and general historical overview of the impact of the global Oil Crisis of 1973. You will note that these paragraphs are not referenced, as what is being presented is generally undisputed historical fact, which does not need to be referenced (see Chapter 8). However, if the student had decided to quote a particular commentator on this event, then a citation and reference would have been necessary.

In paragraphs ten and eleven, the student moves from a general overview to some specific and referenced statistical detail to back up the statements concerning the working lives of both men and women. Look at the end of paragraph eleven and see how the student uses the final sentence to lead into the discussion in paragraph twelve, and to analyse the meaning behind the statistic presented: 'The traditional idea of abandonment of career at marriage, or when children arrive (if they do), is still an option today, but it is one among many'.

The student engages with the second part of the essay task in paragraphs twelve to fourteen and presents a summary of the impact of work changes on the lives of both men and women. There is a sense of the student's 'own voice' emerging with the interpretation presented: 'These choices can be said to mirror values inherent in a service sector dominated economy: the importance of "choices", "quality" (of life) and "value for money" ' (paragraph 14).

10.2.4 Own voice

As it is not referenced, the expression 'can be said' can be regarded as the view of the student. Or perhaps it was one read or heard in the past and which has stayed in the student's mind. We are influenced by ideas all the time – this is how we learn – and it can sometimes be difficult, if not impossible, to reference all sources that have influenced us. We cannot always remember where we read, heard, or discussed a particular idea. This type of statement is likely to be a fusion of what someone has written or said, and the student's own viewpoint. If the student could identify specifically **who** had expressed this particular idea, then the author could be cited and referenced. But in an otherwise well referenced essay, most tutors will appreciate that such an unreferenced statement is a genuine attempt by a student to express his or her own ideas, or to interpret events in their own way – and will not accuse them of plagiarism.

10.2.5 Ending well

In the final paragraph we have the **conclusion** to the essay, and the student summarizes and emphasizes key points made in the essay: 'Life choices have now become more individualised and consumer choice driven. As we have seen, commentators could once comfortably describe "typical" situations and could predict "typical" futures. But we cannot do that any more'. The final sentence presents an unequivocal statement that could be challenged. But this is the point of doing it: it gives us something to think about, as well as to end the essay with a flourish.

10.2.6 Style

The final sentence also gave us a sense of the student's style of writing in action. But there were other occasions when the careful 'academic' style gave way to the more personal. You may have noted these:

like the elements today – global warming being a good example – the interventionist hand of Man can change the predictable to the unpredictable

(paragraph 8)

So out with the old in with the new, literally, as many older workers in all sectors of the economy, but particularly from manufacturing, began to be propelled into redundancy or cajoled into taking early retirement

(paragraph 9)

Do I wish to remain single, co-habit, marry – and establish a family in any of these contexts? Will my future life planning be burdened by a mortgage on a house or would I rather manage by renting? How will I live my life post 60 years?

(paragraph 14)

Students often play safe and present their writing entirely in a way they perceive to be 'academic'. But these examples of more personalized writing are welcomed by most tutors, as they present short stylistic changes of voice that make for more interesting reading and give a sense of the real person behind the words.

10.3 Developing your own writing style

Studying at university should present a good opportunity for students to develop their own individuality and individual style of writing. But unfortunately this does not always happen. All too often they feel they need to consciously change from writing in clear English to a convoluted writing style they feel is more 'appropriate' for degree study. Maeve O'Connor (1991) gives an example of this form of writing:

> Although solitary under normal prevailing circumstances, racoons may congregate simultaneously in certain situations of artificially enhanced nutrient resource availability.

In plain English, this means that racoons normally feed alone but will group together if food is left especially for them! So why not simply say this?

10.3.1 Overblown prose

Students often feel they have to write in a long-winded way, because, unfortunately, this is a style of writing they may encounter in academic journals. They read some academic articles and set books, and can encounter prose that is overblown and pretentious – prose that baffles rather than enlightens. Unfortunately many of these academic writers have not taken the time to learn ways of writing more effectively; or are not brave enough to dump the jargon in favour of simpler, clearer prose for fear of being labelled 'popularizers'. And because students struggle to understand the meaning behind the fog of words, they often end up copying the same turgid prose and serving it back undigested and misunderstood to their tutors.

10.3.2 The best academic writing

However, academic writing does not need to be convoluted and impenetrable. The best academic writing is fresh, engaging, interesting, and persuasive. It is simple, without being simplistic or patronizing to the reader. What makes it so? It is worth analysing good writing to reveal the essence of its quality.

Exercise

The following extract is taken from the introduction to an essay: *The Benefits of Good Writing: Or Why Does It Matter That Students Write Well?*, written by Rukhsana Ahmad and Katharine McMahon for a report published by the Royal Literary Fund. I suggest you read it through first in order to gain an impression of its style and content. Then read it again more slowly and underline any sections you feel are particularly effective, and why. I suggest too, that you summarize in a sentence what each paragraph is **about**; one test of a good paragraph is whether you can identify easily the main point within it.

At its most beautiful and complex, excellent writing crystallises into art. The lyrical poem, unforgettable play, haunting novel, powerful essay or compelling film are all collections of words. Even when writing neither seeks nor attains artistic status, for many of us it is the familiar and preferred route to self-expression and action. We use the written word to affirm and connect, to protest and defend, demand and proclaim, inform and persuade. Through writing we can explore, understand and formulate elusive and complex ideas, share information and engage in debate. This process does as much to elucidate our own thoughts as it does to communicate them to others.

But the most functional and elementary role of good writing is antecedent to its creative and expressive forms and modes. This resides in good writing's capacity to transmit, interpret and extend our inheritance of learning over the ages, passing it on to future generations with as much clarity and exactitude as possible. This aspect of writing is the most pertinent to teaching and learning within an academic context. It is, therefore, imperative that our universities and institutions of higher education enable students to achieve the highest possible standard of writing.

This chapter will first explore the term 'good writing' and its qualities, and then establish the benefits to the student, the university and the wider community of ensuring that students at all levels can write well. The shadow side will also be explored. What happens to students who lack the confidence, motivation and skills to write effectively – and what are the implications for their degree course, their personal development and for those who teach or study with them?

(Ahmad and McMahon 2006)

Now try and summarize in a sentence what each paragraph is **about**:

Paragraph 1
Paragraph 2
Paragraph 3

Comments on the essay extract

1 **Starting well.** The task of any writer is to gain and keep the attention of the reader. Look at the way the first sentence does this: 'At its most beautiful and complex, excellent writing crystallises into art'. The words 'beautiful' and 'complex' lure us into the text because of their unexpected introduction

into an academic article, and for the juxtaposition of images created by these words. We often have an image of academic writing as dry and lifeless, and words like 'beautiful' can pleasantly surprise us.

The authors remind us that writing can untangle complex ideas and present them in a 'beautiful' way and that attracts and appeals to us aesthetically. The word 'crystallises' is interesting. The authors could have simply said 'changes'. But the word 'crystallises' is a more precise – and elegant – term to use, as it conveys the idea of separate and disparate elements fusing into one attractive, unified form. The use of the word 'art' in relation to 'powerful' academic writing can remind us that our essay need not just be a dull, utilitarian thing, but rather a means of persuasion.

2 **Connecting with our senses**. Throughout the extract the authors carefully choose words which convey action; connect with our senses; or have other emotional resonances. Adjectives such as 'lyrical', 'unforgettable', and 'haunting', add a qualitative dimension to the writing. And action is spurred on through a sense of pace and rhythm produced by using paired or single verbs; for example, 'we use the written word to affirm and connect, to protest and defend, demand and proclaim, inform and persuade'; or 'we can explore, understand and formulate elusive and complex ideas, share information and engage in debate'.

3 **Structure**. Each paragraph introduces and develops a particular idea:

- The first paragraph presents the role of writing as a prerequisite and spur to action.
- The second paragraph reminds us of the role of writing in passing on knowledge to others 'with as much clarity and exactitude as possible'.
- The third paragraph describes the structure of the chapter and highlights important features of it. This raises the interest and anticipation of the reader: note the phrase 'the shadow side will also be explored'; the essay will look into less obvious and darker places and it ends with a rhetorical question.

4 **Rhetorical questions**. Rhetorical questions can be effective in assignments providing you use them sparingly. This you must do, as your role is to answer the questions in assignments and not pose them! However, if you both pose a question **and** attempt to answer it, then this can make for interesting reading, and can demonstrate your depth of reading and your analytical ability. You may have noted the use of rhetorical questions in the example essay shown earlier in this chapter (paragraph 14). The student could not, however, have answered these questions, as they were general life questions that only individuals can answer for themselves.

5 **Not for the likes of me?** Finally, you may think that this was an extract written by professional writers and that you will never be able to write like this yourself. Not true. It certainly takes effort and practice. But you can learn from reading good quality writing, if you analyse the way the writer

has organized and shaped the text, the emotional impact of the words used, and the quality of the arguments presented. I hope you will agree there was no sense of this being an article patched together from the work of others; it was clearly the genuine and original 'voices' of the two authors concerned – even though it was written in the third person. You will know it is good writing if it strikes you as particularly interesting and effective, and if it has connected with you at a deep level. You may not know why, but you know it has. And if it does, then try and identify why.

10.4 You and 'I'

The third person style of writing tends to be the current norm in essay writing in Britain and elsewhere. There is a convention in writing for higher education that arguments should be presented in a dispassionate and objective way. One way of doing this is to try and remove the word 'I' from assignments.

But like most established conventions it is subject to the forces of change and some tutors will encourage students to include their own opinions. Some assignments may, in fact, invite you to relate theories directly to your own personal experiences, thus inviting you to use the term 'I'.

The following assignment title is one such example:

> Organizational change can be a difficult process for all concerned. Describe a situation in which you resisted change. Why did you do so? What were the consequences of your resistance?

In an assignment like this you are being asked to do two things:

1 Demonstrate your knowledge of the dynamics of change, particularly organizational change.
2 Relate this knowledge to your own personal experiences.

In such an assignment you can usually adopt 'two voices':

- The 'detached observer'.
- The 'active participant'.

The 'detached observer' (objective)	The 'active participant' (subjective)
You analyse objectively and discuss the ideas and theories of organizational change, e.g. preparing for change; managing change; sources of resistance.	You make connections between your own personal experiences and the theories, ideas and practices presented in your assignments.

So your assignment can be written reflecting these two voices. There is the voice of the 'detached observer', and your own voice: the 'active participant'. However, your own comments will need to be made in a reflective way and will involve making connections between your own experiences and the theories, ideas, and practices that you have been studying. You would need to ask yourself 'what do my experiences add to this discussion?'

An assignment of this type might be introduced to the reader, as follows:

Example

> This assignment will discuss the nature of innovation and change in organizations and the impact that change can have on the people involved both inside and outside the organization. I will connect this discussion to my own experiences when I worked at a large department store in London that was subject to a merger by a larger retail organization. At the time, I felt the merger was badly managed, in terms of poor communication that preceded and followed the change. I will be discussing this aspect in relation to exploring the implications of my resistance to the change.

To try and avoid the use of the first person term, 'I', in this situation would be clumsy and unnecessary – and don't forget you have been invited to reflect on your own personal experiences. However, you would revert to a more detached and passive voice when switching from the personal to the detached observer.

A 'detached observer' style of writing in the same assignment might look like this:

Example

> Organizational change refers to any transformation in the design or functioning of an organization. It is likely to happen when an organization creates or adopts a method of production or working practice that is different in a significant way from the one preceding it.

10.4.1 Keeping the 👁 out of assignments

As stated earlier there is a convention in higher education that author's ideas should be discussed in a seemingly detached and objective way; 'seemingly', as the selection of evidence to present in an assignment is a subjective act and can reflect the student's own position and preferences.

One way to present ideas in a detached way is to use alternatives to 'I' at these points in an assignment. These can include:

- It can be argued . . .
- Arguably . . .
- This assignment will present the following point of view . . .
- Some commentators, notably Bloggs (1990) and Jones (1992) have argued . . .
- It may be that . . .
- We can see that . . . ('We' in this context refers to anyone who cares to see!)
- This assignment will attempt to show that . . .
- Perhaps . . .
- One point of view is that . . .
- Another point of view suggests however, that . . .
- There are two sides to this question. First . . .
- However, . . .
- In conclusion it can be argued that . . .

Main points from this chapter:

- You will never 'find your own voice' in assignments if you copy and paste from other people's work.
- Don't emulate the convoluted style of writing you can sometimes find in academic articles.
- Good English is always clear and unambiguous.
- If you are drawn to text you sense is 'good writing', try and analyse why it attracts you.
- Be aware of when it is appropriate to write in the first person, and when it is not.
- Learn a range of alternative words or terms to the first person 'I' to use in assignments when an objective voice is needed.

11

Sources of help

Support from tutors • Support from other students • Counselling services • Learning support centres • The LearnHigher network • The 'Write-Now' CETL • The Student Network CETL • The best support is you • Suggested additional reading

This final chapter looks at sources of help available to support you in improving your assignment results and to become a more effective learner. It includes sources of help within your own institution, as well as help from other networks, services, and organisations. Although help is often available, it may not be obvious in a large, sprawling, or disconnected campus.

The emphasis in UK higher education is on encouraging students to be 'independent learners'; but the contrast between support offered in colleges and schools to that in higher education institutions can leave some new students feeling isolated and vulnerable, as shown in these students' comments:

Every emphasis is placed on independent learning. It often comes as a shock to many students the lack of help they receive once they arrive at university. Independent learning requires one working in their own time. It also requires homework and preparation being done for seminars, but often the work will not be checked or even referred to.

Independent learning is a very new and scary concept for new students because they have never been responsible for their own development. The lecturers tell the students the workload and the requirements of learning, but no student really believes everything they are told by their teachers.

(Quoted in Green 2007)

Students now arrive at institutions of higher education from very diverse academic backgrounds, and a significant minority may not have the experience of writing the essays and academic reports that their tutors expect. Many international students, for example, have not had to write essays before or may not have been asked to reference their sources in the way required in Britain. They may also have had very different, and often more mentor-like and close, relationships with their tutors, and can be disappointed to find how distant some of their British tutors are. The result is that many struggle to produce the quality of work expected, because they simply do not understand what is expected of them. A tutor might talk in general terms about the assignment brief, but often what the student needs is someone with the time and patience to explain, or preferably show, what is expected and how to achieve the desired result.

So what support can you expect to find within your chosen institution?

11.1 Support from tutors

Although tutors in Britain often carry a heavier workload in comparison with colleagues in other countries, and can be elusive, they are usually the best people to talk to regarding assignment related difficulties, and in particular to learn in more detail what went wrong. Two postgraduate management studies confirmed this to me:

> I got a 'B' for my assignment. I thought it deserved an 'A' with the amount of time I spent on it [and] felt very disappointed. I had a discussion with the Lecturer to see where I went wrong. It turns out I didn't use enough journal references – instead I relied on web based references too much; I also didn't use enough critical analysis.

> I consulted my lecturers, professors and tutors; if you don't consult them, you insult them.

The importance of talking to tutors about disappointing results has been emphasized in a number of studies (see Norton 1990; Burke 2006; Carless 2006). However, students can be reluctant to do this, often fearing that the tutor will be off-hand with them, or because they feel it is better to keep a low profile, not admit to a problem, and hope for a better mark next time. But talking to course and personal tutors about your results is definitely a smart move towards improving assignment grades.

Zeegers and Giles (1996), for example, found that biology undergraduate students who were awarded a high mark in an essay assignment had often discussed the work beforehand with a member of the department staff. There were other factors involved too, but students who speak to a tutor about an assignment usually do so to clarify issues, or to gain clues or advice on specific directions to take in an assignment. This can pay off for them.

If you are required to contact your tutor by email in order to arrange a meeting, do ensure that you write in a clear and literate way. Nothing infuriates tutors more to receive this type of email correspondence:

> Hiya id like a meeting with u to talk about my cse work reslt next week is ok for me on monday im free at 10 or 2. look 4wood to hearing from u
> J Smith

Most of your tutors will receive over 30 email messages a day. To encourage them to read yours, ensure that you state the topic clearly and succinctly in the subject line, e.g. 'Request for an appointment'. In the first line of your text, state the point and purpose of writing. Keep sections of writing short and have a space between sections. Above all, your email should prompt, in a courteous way, some action from the tutor. State clearly, but reasonably, what you would like them to do, and the timescale involved. Make sure you include your full name and UB number at some point, and include the title of the module in question, if relevant. In a formal email do not use abbreviations; it is not a text message. The following is an example of the type of email correspondence tutors like to receive:

Example

Request for an appointment

Dear Dr Jones

   I would like to arrange a meeting with you to discuss my coursework for the xyz module. I was disappointed with my result and would like to learn more about the issues you raised in the feedback, to help me avoid the same problems in the future.

I have free periods next Monday (14th) at 10am or 2pm, or Wednesday (16th) after 12pm, or Thursday (17th) between 10am and 12pm.

I look forward to hearing from you with confirmation as to which of these times is most convenient for you. If none of these is possible for you, I would be grateful if you could suggest some other times.

Thank you.
(Mr) John Smith UB 00876000

However, there may be occasions when speaking to or corresponding with the course or module tutor does not lead to a resolution of the problem. For example, you may perceive the tutor's attitude to be high-handed or unhelpful. These situations are rare, but they can happen. If you find yourself in this situation do not be afraid to approach the tutor's immediate senior colleagues. This may seem a formidable thing to do, particularly if you are new to the whole experience of higher education, but do not be afraid to do it. You need to gain answers to your questions about why you did not do well, otherwise you will be frustrated and increasingly disillusioned by your experiences in higher education.

One student who contacted me had approached the course administration office after receiving a series of negative comments from her tutor. She wrote to me:

I think the build up of sarcastic remarks over several assignments got to me so when assignment four arrived covered in red ink I felt so upset by it that I rang the office to ask for another copy of the next assignment to redo it. In fact, I was quickly put through to a senior tutor. They then rang my tutor, which I hadn't wanted, but she emailed me, in effect with an apology, and thereafter was more careful with her remarks in assignments and in tutorials.

However, if you are wary about taking matters a stage further beyond an obstructive tutor, you could enlist the support of your student union so you can have the backing of your peers in any approach made to senior management.

11.2 Support from other students

Most of the students I contacted in researching this book had also drawn on help available from other sources, particularly the support of their peers. One student wrote of the help he gained eventually from his friends in the class: 'When I read [the feedback] comment that I failed to really address the question ... I asked my intelligent classmates about the subject before I did the next assignment, and also when the assignment involved calculations, I checked the answers with them ... and it helped with improving my assignments'.

There is no doubt that student-to-student support can be a very effective way of learning. Try and find another student on the same course (a '**study buddy**') and meet up regularly to talk through the main points from a lecture, seminar, or set reading. You can, for example, share out reading with a study buddy in a 'jigsaw' approach to learning. This involves both students agreeing to read half of a book chapter and then sharing its contents with each other.

Another variation on this is to form a **study group**, which involves a group meeting on a regular basis and agreeing in advance on an agenda. You could, for example, agree to review a particular lecture, read a selected chapter of a set book, or work on an essay together. You could take it in turns to start off the agreed discussion and use group brainstorming methods to bring ideas to the surface. Talking to other people about a subject requires you to organize your thoughts into a logical sequence. You also have to take into account the other people's knowledge of the subject, and ability level, which makes you refine the way you communicate with them.

Many institutions now organize **peer assisted learning or mentoring programmes** to formalize student-to-student support, and it is worth finding out if there is such a scheme at your university or college. Typically, such a scheme will involve experienced students helping new students, particularly in their first semester. The new student (or mentee) is likely to meet the more experienced student (the mentor) on a regular basis, either one-to-one, or in a small group. The mentor is not a 'teacher' and does not do the mentee's work for them, but instead offers advice and the benefit of their experience. Four student mentors spoke of their experiences about mentoring new students:

> We are able to advise them on points which lecturers might not explain or even cover, such as expected layout and font sizes regarding their assignments.

> I had to learn how to Harvard reference myself last year, which I found hard to grasp, so I thought giving the students some basic advice on referencing would be of use.

> On going through a list of academic skills provided by their tutor, we worked through each point, explaining it in colloquial language so it appeared nowhere as bad as it looked.

> By hearing from someone who has just been through what they are about to start, we can give a more honest and realistic view of what they need to be doing outside university hours.
>
> (Quoted in Green 2007)

The advantage of these schemes for a new student is that they can ask questions more easily of their peers and also begin to form friendship networks with both new and experienced students. The mentors inevitably cut through the jargon and explain things in straightforward and clear ways to their mentees. The mentors gain too. They gain the satisfaction of helping others, they gain useful skills to put on their CV, and they also gain by explaining a subject to another person – in the process they are sharpening and reinforcing their own knowledge.

11.3 Counselling services

All institutions of higher education will have a counselling service to give you an opportunity to talk in confidence about your own personal sense of disappointment in poor assignment results. A counsellor will encourage you to talk about your feelings and responses to the situation, and will also help you to move forward, practically and emotionally, and to become more resilient with any future setbacks.

11.4 Learning support centres

Most institutions of higher education now provide learning support services for students and these can come under different titles. They may be labelled 'learner development units', 'study skills centres', 'effective learning services', or 'academic support centres'. Some institutions of higher education have also established units specifically to help students develop their abilities with both spoken and written English, and these may be called 'language units', 'communication workshops', or 'writing centres' (see below in section 11.6, 'Write Now').

These units may be a part of the library service or administratively separate from it, but the university library is certainly the best place to find out what is available and where you can access study support. These learning support units often produce booklets and leaflets on aspects of learning, such as writing essays, referencing, time management, and so on, and most offer regular effective learning workshops. One student wrote to me to describe how she used these resources after receiving disappointing results:

> Offence was the only defence I had; either come up with the way of success or just pack the bags and leave. So I started with the handbooks available from the school on essay writings, effective writing, and time management.

These units usually operate on a drop-in or interview basis, and offer advice on effective learning techniques, for example on how to write well structured and well organized assignments, make better notes, manage your time, give good presentations, and so on. They also give you an opportunity to talk through any learning related difficulties you may be having, for example problems with getting started with writing an assignment, anxiety about exams or working in groups, and other potentially stressful situations.

However, what most will **not** do is proofread assignments to highlight spelling and grammatical errors, although they will often be willing to look at selected parts of any assignment to try and highlight any recurring errors. They can, however, refer you to agencies or individuals willing to proofread assignments (see Chapter 9).

11.5 The LearnHigher network

There are thousands of individual Internet sites available where learning support resources and materials are available to become a more effective learner. However, 16 institutions of higher education in England have formed a **LearnHigher** network to help you find the best quality, mainly electronic, resources in the following learning areas:

- Academic writing.
- Assessment.
- Critical thinking and reflecting.
- Doing research.
- Group work.
- Independent learning / self-directed study.
- Information literacy.
- Listening and interpersonal skills.
- Learning for all (inclusivity).
- Mobile learning.
- Numeracy, maths, and statistics.
- Oral communication.
- Personal development planning.
- Problem solving and creative thinking.
- Reading and note making.
- Referencing.
- Report writing.
- Time management.
- Understanding organizations.
- Visual practices.

Many of these institutions have identified gaps in the resources currently available and have produced material to bridge the gap, but they also help you gain access to high quality material and resources produced by other institutions and organizations. The main **LearnHigher** website is a 'one-stop-shop' to find these resources (see: www.learnhigher.ac.uk).

The **LearnHigher** network is known as a Centre of Excellence in Teaching and Learning (CETL), and is one of 74 collaborative UK networks of higher education institutions established in 2005 to encourage institutions to evaluate and share good practice in teaching and learning. Many CETLs are aimed at academic staff, but a number, like **LearnHigher**, offer resources and support for both students and higher education staff. Here are two other examples of CETLs that you might like to check out, as their goals connect with the aims of this book.

11.6 The 'Write-Now' CETL

The **Write Now** CETL is a collaborative network of three universities in England to help students develop their confidence and abilities as writers, both generally and in particular for assignment purposes. An important emphasis of their work is to help students find their 'own voices' in assignments (see Chapter 10 of this book).

Write Now initiatives include the establishment of writing centres and a writing mentor scheme. They have also produced a very useful guide for students entitled, *What I Wish I Knew in My First Year About . . . Writing Essays at University* (available at: www.writenow.ac.uk/assessmentplus). This includes quotes from students on their experiences of learning at degree level.

11.7 The Student Network CETL

The **Student Network** CETL brings together students and staff of higher education to help give students an opportunity to get involved in all the other CETL initiatives, so giving them more of a say in how they are taught and assessed. (More information can be found at: www.heacademy.ac.uk/ourwork/networks/cetls/studentnetwork).

11.8 The best support is you

Finally, the best source of support in the long term is you. You may remember from Chapter 1 that one of the 'fight back' strategies adopted by students who were badly disappointed with their results was through self-analysis. One effective way of doing this is to keep a learning journal. A learning journal is a collection of notes, observations, thoughts, and other relevant materials built up over a period of time; it usually accompanies a period of study, a placement experience, or fieldwork.

Learning journals are an excellent way of reviewing what, how, and why you learned; how you felt about what you learned; and what you can do with the knowledge gained in the future.

However, this seem may like one of those worthy ideas that you might in principle agree with, but in practice ignore. Keeping a learning journal is an extra effort for you in a busy schedule, so why bother?

The answer is that the act of writing will help you to clarify your thoughts and emotions, and help you to focus on your development. It forces you to analyse your feelings about a particular experience:

- *I didn't like the lecture – **WHY?** Was it the lecturer I didn't like – or the topic – or both?*
- *The group is not working well together – **WHAT'S HAPPENING?***
- *I really enjoyed that project – **WHY THIS PROJECT?***
- *It was an interesting topic – **WHY? WHAT MADE IT SO?***

Learning journals only really work if you move away from just **describing** what happened to **analysing** what happened and how you felt about what was happening. The reason for analysing your feelings is that feelings can affect actions, which can affect outcomes.

A learning journal does not have to be a burden or a chore. You can keep it simple, with just two headings in your notebook:

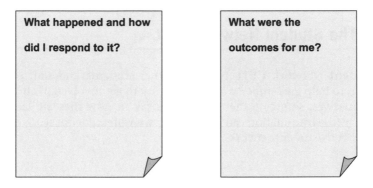

What happened and how did I respond to it?

What were the outcomes for me?

Learning journals are a way for you to record and think about the range of elements involved in any learning situation. There is no standardized format and no one right way of writing a journal. A journal could be a hand written notebook, a word processed document, or it can be recorded verbally on a tape. The important thing is what goes in it. Here is an extract from a learning journal to accompany a career decision making module:

Example: extract from a learning journal

What happened and my response

Watched a video entitled 'Job Interviews' in class today. It pointed out that few people are really prepared and how few take the trouble to even find out about the organization. Although the acting in the video was very staged and corny, it did at least illustrate the basic sequence of events that take place in interviews and pointed out some of the important do's and don'ts of interviewing.

Outcomes

The class discussion was lively today. I think the subject challenged some of our deep fears about rejection and it made many of us a little uncomfortable. I enjoyed it, though, and I think I will keep in mind some of the ideas on how to confront, accept, and manage fear as I prepare for interviews someday.

My big fear in an interview would be that my anxiety would either make me babble on, or take me the other way and make me dry up completely when asked a question. It is the aspect of being judged by others, being weighed up, and dismissed, or accepted, that makes me anxious, and if I am honest rather resentful too about being in this subservient position.

Interviews are a bit of a power game, it seems to me, although I can see why they are still one of the main ways of selecting people. Employers need to see if you will 'fit in', and that's why it's important to try and get an idea of the values of the company beforehand, and not just think about the job.

In this journal extract the student:

- **Describes** what happened during the class.
- **Criticizes** aspects of the learning medium, e.g. the video.
- **Summarizes** what he or she learned – from both subject knowledge and self-knowledge perspectives.
- **Reflects on** what he or she enjoyed about the class.
- **Offers** a personal response to the class discussion.
- **Expresses** his or her fears at two levels: **describes** them and **analyses** them. Being aware of these deeper feelings may encourage the student to explore them further. When we do this we are truly effective learners.

The key elements of writing effective learning journals – and for improving your future assignment results are:

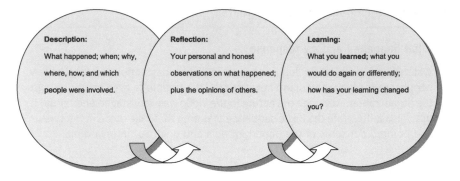

Good luck with your future assignments.

11.9 Suggested additional reading

The following sources will develop and extend the discussion of issues and ideas raised in this book.

Cottrell, S. (2005) *Critical Thinking Skills: Developing Effective Analysis and Argument*. Basingstoke: Palgrave MacMillan.

De Bono, E. (1996) *Teach Yourself to Think*. London: Penguin.

Levin, P. (2004) *Write Great Essays!* Maidenhead: Open University Press.

Neville, C. (2007) *The Complete Guide to Referencing and Avoiding Plagiarism*. Maidenhead: Open University Press/McGraw Hill.

Norton, L. et al. (2007) *What I Wish I Knew in My First Year About Writing Essays at University*. London: Assessment Plus (CETL consortium). Available at: www.writenow.ac.uk/assessmentplus (accessed 15 Nov. 2007).

Northedge, A. et al. (1997) *The Sciences Good Study Guide*. Milton Keynes: The Open University.

Appendix 1

Exercise from Chapter 2

All these assessment criteria are important. However, tutors put particular marking emphasis on them in the order shown. So, while 'Accurate use of English/spelling' is important, and may carry a particular percentage of the overall marks, e.g. 10 per cent, more emphasis (and weight of marks) would be placed on the first item: 'Answering the question'.

Criteria	Rank
Clear structure and organization	5
Answers the question	1
Accurate use of English	9
Effective presentation and writing style	6
Demonstrates understanding of the subject	2
Evidence and demonstration of wide reading	8
Relevant information is selected and used in the assignment	4
There is a clear point of view or 'argument'	3
Evaluation of evidence (ability to identify strengths and weaknesses of what you read)	6

Comments on the exercise

1 *Answers the question.* This item is usually at the top of all tutors' assessment criteria lists, no matter what the subject area. It is easy to get carried away when writing an essay or a report. You may want to demonstrate your knowledge to the tutor by writing all you know, but it is definitely the wrong strategy. Stay focused on the question or task.

2 *Demonstrates understanding of the subject.* You do this, not by copying other people's words, but by interpreting, summarizing, or paraphrasing the ideas that you encounter.

3 *There is a clear point of view or argument.* This is about having a definite point of view that is easy to identify in your assignment, or about putting forward a convincing case to support a position taken.

4 *Relevant information is selected.* This is about selecting the most reliable evidence to support a particular point of view, and ensuring that it is

referenced accurately. Reliable evidence is often that which has been subjected to the critical scrutiny of others before it is published or appears on the Internet, e.g. peer reviewed journals; government agencies.

5 *Clear structure and organization.* You might know what you want to say, but if you cannot organize your ideas and present them in a well structured way, you are in danger of losing marks. Your tutor wants to be able to read your assignment easily and in a linear way: it should have a clear introduction, with the ideas in paragraphs or sections 'cascading' logically from one to the other, leading to a conclusion.

6 *Evaluation of evidence / Effective presentation and writing style.* The tutors in the survey put equal weight on these two. Evaluation of evidence is about trying to weigh up the merits and flaws of your reading or other sources, so that you can make qualitative judgements about them, including whether or not they should be included in your assignment. Effective writing style is about communicating clearly with the tutor, and about finding 'your voice' (see Chapter 10). Developing your own writing style will not happen if you copy and patch together bits from other people's work.

7 *Evidence and demonstration of wide reading.* Although this appears to be toward the end of the list, it really underpins many of the higher ranked items and tutors are certainly interested in how widely you have read around the subject. This is usually indicated by your selection, evaluation, and referencing of the evidence you present. Tutors are often impressed if you find and summarize reliable and relevant information from outside the recommended reading lists.

8 *Accurate use of English.* Compared with the mortal offence of not answering the question, weak grammar and poor spelling is, relatively speaking, a minor sin! However, accurate use of English, including sound grammar and spelling, will undoubtedly brighten your tutor's day. Conversely, an assignment full of spelling mistakes and grammatical errors can be another nail in your assignment coffin, if combined with other problems.

Appendix 2

In Chapter 3 there were four examples of assignment titles or tasks. You were asked to identify the key words, any propositions or assumptions, and to summarize the approach or broad direction you would take in each example.

Example 1

> It can be said that the longstanding nature–nurture argument about the development of human behaviour still rages today. Some theorists take the position that behaviour is attributable to genetic factors, while others argue that environmental factors are responsible. Explore this issue, with reference to relevant theorists and commentators.

1 *Key words*: 'Nature–nurture argument', 'genetic factors', 'environmental factors', these all need to be briefly defined or explained. 'Explore': means to identify and explain the main features of the topic under discussion, including any main theories, ideas, models, or practices.
2 *Propositions/assumptions*: 'It can be said that the longstanding nature–nurture argument about the development of personality still rages today'. Yes, 'it can be said', but is it true? You would need to discuss this proposition, and in particular examine to what extent these views are over-simplified polarities, shaped by external political or other social factors, and if there has been a convergence of views on both sides.
3 *What's expected of you*: Define terms (also see key words above); introduce arguments on both sides; look at the influence of other disciplines, e.g. philosophy, politics, cultural studies, on the 'debate', and to what extent, and in which areas, there has been a convergence of views. You would need to look, for example, at the relationship and dynamics between nature and nurture and how one can affect the other.

Example 2

> What is the difference between a conductor and an insulator? Give experimental evidence for the descriptions that you give, and try to account for these descriptions using a microscopic model of the material.

1 *Key words*: You need to define terms 'conductor' and 'insulator'; and the term 'experimental evidence' suggests you need to look for research studies to help you identify the differences; 'account' means to explain and reach a conclusion; and 'microscopic model' gives you a precise task specification.
2 *Propositions/assumptions*: It assumes there *is* a difference between a conductor and an insulator.
3 *What's expected of you?* To distinguish between conductors and insulators by identifying and explaining the distinguishing characteristics of each and by using research evidence to support your explanation; and reach a conclusion using a microscopic model of the material.

Example 3

> 'History is more or less bunk. It's tradition. We don't want tradition. We want to live in the present, and the only history that is worth a tinker's damn is the history that we make today.' (Henry Ford 1916). Discuss.

1 *Key words*: 'History', 'bunk', 'tradition', 'live in the present', 'tinker's damn', and 'Henry Ford 1916'. You would need to think about the meanings of the words, who said them (Henry Ford), when, and the relationship between the words used, e.g. 'history' and 'tradition'.
2 *Propositions/assumptions*: Strong propositions are used here. History is equated as 'bunk' (rubbish) and equated with tradition, and that we should live for today.
3 *What's expected of you?* Briefly explain the context of the remark: who Henry Ford was, and the fast-changing industrial pace and political disruption of the period. However, the main discussion would be around definitions of history and tradition, the role of history in contemporary life, relationship of history to tradition, and the role of tradition and contemporary action.

Example 4

> Evaluate the concerns that, for all the talk of a new flexible workforce, the reality is somewhat more contradictory and problematic.

1 *Key words*: The words 'for all the talk' and 'new', and, 'somewhat more', suggest that the idea of a 'flexible workforce' has been presented by some commentators in a positive way. The second part of the title suggests, however, that the 'reality' is 'contradictory' and 'problematic'. 'Contradictory' is a useful clue to the fact that research on the topic tends to throw up more questions than answers! The term 'problematic' suggests there have been difficulties introducing or servicing flexible work practices – or both. You are asked to 'evaluate' this 'reality'. The term 'evaluate' means to assess the worth, importance, or usefulness of something, using the evidence available. The word 'reality' is interesting. It is hard to summarize 'reality' at the best of times, let alone in a limited word essay. But it is necessary for you to reach a conclusion, although it is likely to be a somewhat circumspect one.

2 *Propositions/assumptions*: The title also presents us with a proposition: that the 'reality' *is* more 'contradictory and problematic'. So your essay will need to reach some judgement or conclusion on this.

3 *What's expected of you?* You need to define what is meant by flexible work practices; set geographic parameters for your discussion (will there be global, national, regional discussion of issues?); discuss evolution, scale, and current extent of flexible working practices today within geographical parameters selected; and discuss the perceptions and expectations of employers/employees in relation to flexible working, e.g. similarities, tensions, contradictions.

Appendix 3

In Chapter 4 you listed what questions you could ask William Bridges about his four stage theory of change. You may have asked one or more of the following questions.

1 *Methodology*: how did he arrive at his theory? Did he formulate his theory based on research evidence or through other means, e.g. review of own and others' work? If it was based or built on the work of others, who were they, and when were their ideas published? If applicable, how do Bridges' ideas differ from these earlier commentators? Have Bridges' ideas been tested and applied by others, if so, who, where, when, and with what result?
2 *Validity of theory*: must we pass through all the stages advanced by Bridges? Might there be additional stages not proposed by Bridges? If so, what additional stages might you propose to develop the theory?
3 *Sequence*: do we have to go through the stages in the order suggested by Bridges? Can we skip a change? Can we go through a particular stage more than once?
4 *Discretionary and nondiscretionary change*: are Bridges' ideas universally applicable to everyone experiencing change, or more applicable to people who have change forced on them (nondiscretionary change)? How relevant are his ideas to those people who pursue or readily embrace change (discretionary change)?
5 *Cultural issues*: how applicable are Bridges' ideas in a global context? Or are they more relevant to societies in a particular hemisphere or region? If they are not universally applicable, why is this?
6 *Currency*: has Bridges revised the theory since 1980? If so, what is his current thinking? If not, are the ideas still applicable today?
7 *Personal experience*: to what extent does Bridges' theory connect with your own experiences of change?

You could pursue answers to these questions for your assignment – which would move your work from being merely descriptive to analytical.

Appendix 4

In Chapter 5, you were presented with an essay and asked to think about its structure. Two of the boxes in the worksheet: for paragraph six, and for paragraphs eight to ten, were left blank. You were asked to summarize in the blank spaces what the writer was trying to do and say in these paragraphs.

1 **Paragraph six:** presents the main advantages of the Internet for recruitment purposes. This is stated clearly in the opening sentence. Also, examples, properly referenced, are presented to illustrate points made.
2 **Paragraphs eight to ten:** these outline the drawbacks of using the Internet for recruitment purposes. The drawbacks were briefly summarized in paragraph seven, and each of the three following paragraphs focuses on one of the issues raised. Paragraph eight highlights the issue of equality of access to the Internet, pointing out that not everyone has easy access to it; paragraph nine picks up the issue of confidentiality and data protection; whilst ten deals with the numbers of applications received by employers and the issues relating to difficulties encountered by online applicants.

Appendix 5

In Chapter 6, in the 'What's missing?' exercises, you were asked to think about what other elements might be added to both the PEST and SWOT analysis models, to make them more comprehensive in their coverage of issues.

1 **PEST:** political, economic, socio-cultural, and technological dimensions. Another dimension you might add to your analysis is **historical**, particularly in relation to the impact of the recent past on the country or region concerned. History can impact on the other four PEST elements, so it would be useful to consider the impact of the past on the present shape – and likely future direction – of the subject of your enquiry.
2 **SWOT:** strengths, weaknesses, opportunities, and threats. These four elements represent two sets of polarised opposites: strengths–weaknesses; opportunities–threats. There are, however, midway positions that might need to be considered, such as 'ambiguities' or 'uncertainties'. An uncertainty, for example, may not be regarded as a 'threat', but it could become one. Likewise, ambiguities, meaning a lack of clarity (possibly in relation to opportunities), might not be taken into account unless specifically included in an analysis.

Appendix 6

'When to reference' exercise from Chapter 8: responses

Situation	Yes	No
1 When quoting directly from a source.	✓	
2 To give the source of any statistics or other data.	✓	
3 When summarizing what has happened over a period of time, and where there is general agreement by commentators on cause and effect.		X
4 When using definitions available freely in the public domain, e.g. from websites.	✓	
5 When summarizing or paraphrasing what is found on a website, and when no writer, editor, or author name is shown.	✓	
6 When summarizing or paraphrasing what a particular writer or commentator has said on a topic.	✓	
7 When summarizing, e.g. in a concluding section or paragraph, what has been discussed and referenced earlier in your text.		X
8 To show the source of photographs freely available on the Internet and where no named photographer is mentioned.	✓	
9 When using information supplied by your tutor in a course handout.	✓	
10 When stating freely available facts in the public domain about a topic.		X

Additional notes on some of the above situations

(1) The page number should also be included in the intext citation or main source reference.

(3) This is an example of common knowledge (see Chapter 8). However, if a single source, e.g. a history book, is used, it would be wise to cite and reference this.

(5)   The name of the website should be cited and referenced if no named author or writer is shown for the item in question.

(8)   This would apply also to graphs, charts, tables, and other graphic illustrations.

(9)   This is work produced by another person, i.e. your tutor. If you use it in your assignment, you need to cite and reference the source. This would include the name of the tutor, year, title of handout, module title, and name of institution.

(10)   This is another example of common knowledge, see above (3).

Plagiarism awareness exercise

In Chapter 8 you were also invited to decide which of the following scenarios amounted to plagiarism.

1   *There is a set of statistics on a freely available government website. You use them in your assignment, but forget to include the source in your references.* **Yes – plagiarism.** You should always reference the source of any statistics that you include in your assignment. If you do not, you could be accused of plagiarism and the reason that you 'forgot' to do it would sound a weak defence. You would be expected to know that you should reference your sources in this situation – and not forget to do it.

2   *You see a useful article on an Internet site. You copy 50 percent of the words and add 50 percent in your own words. You don't include a source, as no author's name is shown on the site.* **Yes – plagiarism.** Most institutions of higher education in Britain will want you to either summarize or paraphrase what you read, or treat an extract from a source as a quotation. The rationale for this is that the process of summarizing and paraphrasing helps students to gain a deeper level of understanding about a topic. By converting the ideas into a choice of your own words, you have to think harder about them and are thus more likely to gain a deeper level of knowledge. For this reason this 'patchwork' approach to writing would be regarded as plagiarism by many of your tutors. The lack of a citation and reference would be an aggravating factor in this situation. The fact that no author's name is shown is irrelevant; in a case like this you would summarize or paraphrase in your own words and cite and reference the name and details of the website.

3   *You find an interesting black and white illustration on a website. You copy and paste it into your assignment, and don't include the designer or artist's name, as none is shown on the site.* **Yes – plagiarism.** You should always reference the source of any illustrations, including

photographs, charts, graphs, and other graphics. If no designer, artist, or originator's name is shown, you should cite and reference the name of the website.

4 *You are researching the impact of an historical event. You want to write a paragraph on what actually happened to include as background material in your assignment. You look at three reference books and they all say much the same thing on the cause of the problem. You summarize this in your own words, but do not reference the books you consulted.*
No – not plagiarism. It is not plagiarism to summarize what has happened in the past, providing you draw from a range of sources and there is no significant dispute between commentators on the events you describe. This would be regarded as 'common knowledge'. However, if you just use one source, or you quote directly, or paraphrase, from any particular source, the author(s) should be cited and referenced.

5 *You find a definition of a concept on an Internet site encyclopedia collaboratively written by its readers (a 'Wiki' site), which you use in your assignment. You do not reference this.* Yes – plagiarism. You should reference the source of all definitions that would not be regarded as 'common knowledge', e.g. concepts and specialist terms. If no particular author or writer is shown, then cite and reference the name of the site. But you should bear in mind that tutors often discourage the use of such sites as sources in assignments and often prefer that you use primary sources for definitions and other descriptive text (see Chapter 7).

6 *You copy something from a course handout given to you by your tutor that contains secondary source information, i.e. the tutor has summarized the work of others. You do not reference this.* Yes – plagiarism. You would either cite and reference the name of the tutor concerned or read the primary sources the tutor has summarized and reference these – preferably the latter.

7 *You are part of a study group of six. You pair up and each pair agrees to write a third of the assignment and then pool the work. All the members of the group then submit the collated assignment individually.* Yes – plagiarism. Study groups are an excellent way to share ideas and to learn. However, if you are asked to submit an individual assignment this is what you have to do. This scenario is an example of collaboration in plagiarism, and all members of the group would be implicated.

8 *You include the expression 'Children should be seen and not heard' in your essay without a source reference.* No – not plagiarism. This is an example of an aphorism, or a common saying, and it would not be plagiarism to use it as such an example in an assignment. You would not need to show the exact source. It would be a good practice, however, to show an approximate period of origin in the text of your essay, e.g. fifteenth century proverb.

9   *You have a conversation with a classmate about an essay assignment. She or he has an interesting perspective on the topic, which makes you think. You decide to use this idea; no reference is included in your essay.* **No – not plagiarism.** Only **work** can be plagiarized. 'Work' is when ideas are presented, manifested, or published into the public domain in some way, e.g. book, article, Internet, play, film, painting, sculpture, dance performance, etc. We are influenced by ideas all the time; this is how we learn. We think about ideas and may convert them to our own advantage in some way. If, however, your classmate had converted the ideas into **work** and presented it into the public domain in some way, then that would be a different matter. Also, if your classmate had written an essay and allowed you to copy all, or part of this, into your own assignment, then you would be both implicated in plagiarism.

10 *You have been told that your assignment essay must be 'all your own work'. However, you are worried about your spelling and grammar so you pay a proofreader to check your work. The proofreader suggests changes to sentences throughout the essay to help the meaning becoming clearer to a reader. You accept these changes and submit the assignment.*
    No – not plagiarism. In this example the proofreaders is not changing the nature of the ideas presented in the assignment, but just helping you to express these ideas more clearly. This is not plagiarism. This book, for example, will have gone through a number of proofreading filters before you read it – to identify spelling and grammatical errors, and to make the meaning of sentences as transparent as possible to you. It is still my own work, but made clearer, I hope, to you. However, be cautious when asking others to proofread for you. A professional proofreader will only suggest ways of changing the construction of sentence, and not the idea expressed within it. They may, for example, invite you to clarify the point you are making in a particular sentence.

    But if you ask a friend or classmate to look through your work, they can certainly help you to identify spelling and grammatical errors, but do not allow them to change the meaning of a sentence, otherwise you could both stray into 'plagiarism territory.' Instead, ask them to comment on what you are saying, make suggestions perhaps, but then decide for yourself if you want to make the changes suggested. In this way you keep control of the writing; it is still your work. There is more information on the role of proofreaders in Chapter 9.

Appendix 7

Here are comments and answers for exercises from Chapter 9.

Exercise: What's wrong with these sentences?

1 *The University of XYZ is holding it's first 'Plagiarism Awareness Week' in February (13th–17th).* **Comment:** no apostrophe should be used with 'its' in this context, as it is being used here to denote possession.

2 *Its estimated that more than a thousand people were affected by the radiation leak.* **Comment:** the apostrophe should be used to indicate that 'it is' is being shortened to 'it's'.

3 *The CV's were'nt particularly impressive, I'm afraid.* **Comment:** (a) no apostrophe should be used with CVs, as plural, rather than possession is meant here; (b) the apostrophe should be used to replace the missing letter, so 'were'nt' should be 'weren't'; (c) a comma is necessary after 'impressive'.

4 *The report was logical, short, and reading it was easy.* **Comment:** a comma was necessary after 'logical' and 'short'.

5 *The decision to introduce computers has already been made by the Director's.* **Comment:** an apostrophe should not be used, as 'Directors' was being used here in a plural sense.

6 *I decided not to take out the insurance policy on principle because its too expensive.* **Comment:** same as for example 2.

7 *I have devised a plan to ensure our place in the top ten SME's in the region.* **Comment:** same as for example 5.

8 *The BBCs response to the MPs criticism was to invite the MPs to take part in a televised broadcast on the topic.* **Comment:** an apostrophe should be used to denote possession, e.g. BBC's response and MP's criticism.

Exercise: word meanings

Affect: the influence of	**Effect:** the impact of
Ascent: climb	**Assent:** agree
Cited: referenced	**Sited:** located
Complement: goes alongside	**Compliment:** praise
Ordinance: a decree	**Ordnance:** artillery
Precedence: priority	**Precedents:** established course of action
Principal: most important; head of	**Principle:** a standard or value
Stationary: not moving	**Stationery:** paper and related products

Exercise: Reducing the word count

Example 1

The dollar has been declining in value against the euro over the last six years, hurting travellers to Europe and American consumers purchasing European goods. The strengthening euro has not had the expected beneficial impact in Europe, as trade with North America has shown a downward trajectory as a result.
                                              (50 words)
	The dollar has been declining in value against the euro over the last six years, hurting travellers to Europe and American consumers purchasing European goods.
	
	                              (25 words)

Example 2

A new analysis of online consumer data (ComScore 2008) shows that large web companies are learning about the tastes and preferences of people from what they search for and do on the Internet. The data from the search engines of Internet users is routinely gathered and analysed and knowledge gained by the web companies about the things that users are most interested in.
                                              (63 words)
	A new analysis of online consumer data (ComScore 2008) shows that large web companies are learning about the tastes and preferences of people from what they search for and do on the Internet.
	
	                              (33 words)

Example 3

The public's knowledge of health is poor and more government funding for health education is needed. Increased sums of money should be spent on courses to make people aware of personal health issues. People don't always know what they can do to take care of their health, so further investment is needed in training on health matters. (57 words)	The public's knowledge of health is poor and more government funding for health education is needed. (16 words)

Comments

These are all examples of tautology: repeating the same word or sentence in an unnecessary way. The second sentence in exercise 1 says much as the same as the first and can be cut; in example 3 there are two unnecessary sentences!

Tautology is quite common in assignments. It can arise because of student anxiety to make a particular point, leading to a repetition or over emphasis of it. A useful adage in writing is 'less is more' !

References

Ahmad, R. and McMahon, K. (2006) The benefits of good writing: or why does it matter that students write well? *Writing Matters*. London: Royal Literary Fund. Available at: www.rlf.org.uk/fellowshipscheme/research.cfm (accessed 5 Feb. 2007).

Angélil-Carter, S. (2000) *Stolen Language? Plagiarism in Writing*. Harlow: Pearson Education.

Bernard, M., Mills, M., Peterson, M. and Storrer, K. (2001) A comparison of popular online typefaces: which is best and when? *Usability News*, 3(2). Available at: http://psychology.wichita.edu/surl/usabilitynews/3S/font.htm (accessed 10 Dec. 2007).

Bridges, W. (1980) *Transitions: Making Sense of Life's Changes*. Jackson, TN: Perseus Books.

Buchan, J.C., Norris, J. and Kuper, H. (2005) Accuracy of referencing in the ophthalmic literature, *American Journal of Ophthalmology*, 140(6): 1146–8.

Burke, D. (2006) *Sharpen Up Your Skills*. Wolverhampton: University of Wolverhampton. Available at: http://asp.wlv.ac.uk/Level4.asp?UserType=11andlevel4=3961 (accessed 23 Aug. 2007).

Campion, M. (1997) Rules for references: suggested guidelines for choosing literary citations for research articles in applied psychology, *Personnel Psychology*, 50(1): 165–8.

Carless, D. (2006) Differing perceptions in the feedback process, *Studies in Higher Education*, 31(26): 219–33.

Clanchy. J. and Ballard, B. (1998) *How to Write Essays: A Practical Guide for Students*, 3rd edn. Melbourne: Longman.

Chanock, K. (2000) Comments on essays: do students understand what tutors write? *Teaching in Higher Education*, 5(1): 95–105.

Coleman, A. and Chiva, A. (1991) *Coping with Change: Focus on Retirement*. London: Health Education Authority.

ComScore (2008) Press release. Available at: www.comscore.com/press/release.asp?press=2119 (accessed 20 Apr. 2008).

Evans, H. (2000) *Essential English for Journalists, Editors and Writers*. London: Pimlico.

Giles, K. and Hedge, N. (1998) *The Manager's Good Study Guide*. Maidenhead: Open University Press.

Gosling, C., Cameron, M. and Gibbons, P. (2004) Referencing and quotation accuracy in four manual therapy journals, *Manual Therapy*, 9(1): 36–40.

Green, A. (2007) *Peer Assisted Learning: Empowering First Year Engagement With a Formal Curriculum Through the Educative*. Bournemouth: Bournemouth University, Centre for Academic Practice.

Handy, C. (1994) *The Empty Raincoat: Making Sense of the Future*. London: Hutchinson.

Harzing, A. W. (2002). Are our referencing errors undermining our scholarship and credibility? The case of expatriate failure rates, *Journal of Organizational Behavior*, Feb., 23(1): 127–48.

Hilsdon, J. (1999) Awareness of language on a BA undergraduate programme, in P. Thompson (ed.), *Academic Writing Development*. Reading: University of Reading.

Hopson, B. and Scally, M. (1999) *Build Your Own Rainbow: A Workbook for Career and Life Management*. Chalford: Management Books.

Hounsel, D. (1984) Essay writing and the quality of feedback, in T. E. Richardson, M. W. Eysenck and D. W. Piper (eds), *Student Learning: Research in Education and Cognitive Psychology*. Milton Keynes: Open University Press, pp. 109–19.

Huws, U. (1996) *Teleworking: An Overview of the Research*. London: Analytical Social and Economic Research Ltd.

Johnson, T. (2007) How do international students engage with learning about study skills in British higher education? Paper delivered at the Adult Learning Development in Higher Education Symposium, Bournemouth.

Neville, C. (2007) *The Complete Guide to Referencing and Avoiding Plagiarism*. Maidenhead: McGraw Hill/Open University Press.

Norton, L. S. (1990) Essay-writing: what really counts? *Higher Education*, 20: 411–42.

Norton, L., Pitt, E., Harrington, K., Elander, J. and Reddy, P. (2007) *What I Wish I Knew in My First Year About Writing Essays at University*. London: Assessment Plus (CETL consortium). Available at: www.writenow.ac.uk/assessmentplus (accessed 15 Nov. 2007).

O'Connor, M. (1991) *Writing Successfully in Science*. London: Taylor & Francis.

Plain English Campaign (2007) *Job Applications Are Full of Mistakes, Says Survey*. Available at: www.plainenglish.co.uk/news.htm (accessed 2 Feb. 2007).

Powell, C. (2007) *A Leadership Primer* (PowerPoint). Available at www.btm.com.au/Web-Site-Resources/Collin%20Powell%20on%20Leadership.ppt#256,3,Slide3 (Accessed 5 Sept. 2008).

Rani, R. (2000) *Counselling Students: A Psychodynamic Approach*. Basingstoke: MacMillan.

Rose, C. (2000) *Master it Faster: How to Learn Faster, Make Good Decisions and Think Creatively*. London: The Industrial Society.

Royal Mail Group (2003) *Typos Cost UK Business Over £700 Million a Year*. Available at: www.news.royalmailgroup.com/news/articlec.asp?id=816andbrand=royal_mail (accessed 1 May 2006).

Sigman, A. (2001) The typeface you choose says as much as the words you write, *Business in Vancouver*, Dec., 632: 4–10.

Skok, W. (2003) A hitch-hiker's guide to learning in higher education, *BEST Practice*, Sept., 4(1).

Taylor, G. (1989) *The Student's Writing Guide for the Arts and Social Sciences*. Cambridge: Cambridge University Press.

Timmers, P. (2000) *Electronic Commerce: Strategies and Models for Business-to-Business Trading*. Oxford: Wiley.

Waytowich, V. L. Onwuegbuzie, A. J. and Jiao, Q. G. (2006) Characteristics of doctoral students who commit citation errors, *Library Review*, 55(3): 195–208.

Young, P. (2000) 'I might as well give up': self-esteem and mature students' feelings about feedback on assignments, *Journal of Further and Higher Education*, 24(3): 409–18.

Zeegers, P. and Giles, L. (1996) Essay writing in biology: an example of effective student learning? *Research in Science Education*, 26(4): 437–59.

Index

Related books from Open University Press
Purchase from www.openup.co.uk or order through your local bookseller

---

THE COMPLETE GUIDE TO REFERENCING AND AVOIDING PLAGIARISM
Colin Neville

- Why is there so much emphasis on citing sources in some written work?
- How can I be sure I am referencing sources correctly?
- What is plagiarism and how do I avoid it?

There is a great deal of emphasis on accurate referencing in written work for university students, and those writing for professional purposes, but little information on the 'when', the 'why', as well as the 'how' of referencing. This book fills that gap, giving clear guidelines on how to correctly cite from external sources, what constitutes plagiarism, and how it can be avoided.

A unique feature of the book is the comparisons it makes between different referencing styles – such as Harvard, APA, MLA and Numerical referencing styles – which are shown side-by-side. This provides a useful guide, for students as they progress through higher education, and particularly for those on combined studies courses – who may be expected to use two, and sometimes three, different referencing styles.

Other special features in the book include:

- Essays demonstrating referencing in action
- Exercises on when to reference, and on what is, and what is not, plagiarism
- A 'Frequently Asked Questions' section on the referencing issues that most often puzzle people
- A detailed guide to referencing electronic sources, and advice on how to choose reliable Internet sites

A Complete Guide to Referencing and Avoiding Plagiarism is essential reading for all students and professionals who need to use referencing to accurately reflect the work of others and avoid plagiarism.

Contents
Preface – Acknowledgements – Referencing – Why reference? – What, when and how to reference – Plagiarism – Referencing styles – Harvard style of referencing – American Psychological Association (APA) and Modern Languages Association (MLA) referencing styles – Numerical referencing styles – Frequently asked questions – Referencing in action: example references – Index.

2007 240pp

ISBN-13: 978 0 335 22089 2 (ISBN-10: 0 335 22089 4) Paperback

ISBN-13: 978 0 335 22090 8 (ISBN-10: 0 335 22090 8) Hardback

GRAMMAR
A FRIENDLY APPROACH

Christine Sinclair

- Do you feel that your writing lets you down?
- Do you have problems turning your thoughts into writing?
- Do you randomly scatter commas throughout your written work and hope for the best?

You are not alone – and this book is just what you need!

This is a grammar book with a difference. It brings grammar to life by giving examples of grammatical problems in the contexts where they arise by including a soap opera. As the characters' grammar improves, so will yours.

It blends a story about three students – Barbara, Kim and Abel – with advice on specific areas of grammar. The characters' story builds throughout the book, but each chapter can be read separately if readers want to focus on specific grammatical issues.

The book examines and clearly explains aspects of grammar, language use and punctuation such as:

- Academic language
- Standard English
- Correct use of tenses
- Active and passive voices
- Sentence construction and punctuation
- When and where to place an apostrophe
- Using grammar checkers

There are exercises to encourage the reader to relate the issues to their own practice and experiences, as well as an extensive glossary which defines the terms that are used throughout the book.

Grammar: A Friendly Approach is based around issues at university but students from schools and colleges will also love this irreverent look at the rules of grammar: Their teachers and tutors will also see rapid and noticeable improvements in students' written work.

Contents
Introduction – Bad language – Mangling and dangling participles – Getting tense with verbs – Active and passive voices – What is the subject? – The complete sentence – Relationships and relatives – How to be offensive with punctuation – Possessive apostrophes and missing letters – Checking the checker – Finale – Glossary – Appendices – Bibliography – Index.

March 2007   144pp
978–0–335–22008–3 (Paperback)   978–0–335–22009–0 (Hardback)

WRITING UP YOUR UNIVERSITY ASSIGNMENTS AND RESEARCH PROJECTS
A PRACTICAL HANDBOOK

Neil Murray and Geraldine Hughes

- What is good academic writing?
- How should I present my written work?
- How can I improve my written work?

Academic writing can be a daunting prospect for new undergraduates and postgraduates alike, regardless of whether they are home or overseas students. This accessible book provides them/students with all they need to know to produce excellent written work.

Based on their many years of experience, the authors have structured the book so as to build students' confidence in their own writing ability whilst at the same time respecting conventional ideas of what is, and what is not, acceptable in the academic domain. To reinforce student learning, the material is presented using a wealth of clear examples, hands-on tasks with answers, and logical sequences that build on earlier chapters. The first two sections of the book address the preparation and writing of assignments and research projects, while the third provides a useful toolkit containing reference materials on areas including punctuation, grammar and academic terminology.

The book includes numerous tips and insights and comprehensively covers issues such as:

- Reading around a new topic
- The need for coherence and how to achieve it
- Structure and organisation
- Plagiarism, quoting and citing sources
- The main sections of a typical research project
- Writing style
- Finding your own voice
- Examiner expectations

Contents
Foreword – A guide to the book's icons: What do they mean? – Part 1: The fundamentals of academic writing – Introduction – What are the key functions in academic writing? – How should I structure my writing? – What do I need to know about writing style? – Approaching your writing project: Tips and strategies – Part 2: Putting together your research project – Understanding the research and writing process – What are the different components of a research project? – . . .And when it's all over: Publishing and presenting your research – Part 3: Toolkit – Punctuation basics: A brief guide to the correct use of punctuation – Glossary of key terms – The academic word list – Appendix – Index.

2008   256pp
978–0–335–22717–4 (Paperback)   978–0–335–22718–1 (Hardback)

WRITING AT UNIVERSITY
A GUIDE FOR STUDENTS
Second Edition

Phyllis Creme and Mary R. Lea

- What is expected of you in university writing?
- What can you do to develop and build confidence in your writing?
- How can you address the variety of written assignments you will encounter in your studies?

Writing at University is a student writing guide with a difference. It provides a deeper understanding of what writing at university is all about, with useful methods and approaches to give you more control over your academic writing.

The book explores both traditional essay and other kinds of writing that you will need to do as part of your studies. You are encouraged to build upon your existing abilities as a writer through applying practical tasks to your own work.

The second edition of this best-selling title has been completely updated with new coverage of report writing, learning journals, electronic writing and using the internet.

This book is an essential tool for anyone who wants to improve their writing skills at university or FE colleges, including both undergraduates and postgraduate students. It is key reading for students in courses that require essay, report, or dissertation writing and for students returning to study. It is also an invaluable resource for academic staff who want to support students with their writing.

Contents
You and university writing – First thoughts on writing assignments – Writing for different courses – Beginning with the title – Reading as part of writing – Organizing and shaping your writing – Putting yourself into your academic writing – Putting it together – Completing the assignment and preparing for next time – Using different kinds of writing – Using learning journals and other exploratory writing – References – Index.

160pp   0 335 21325 1 (Paperback)